EVIDENCE GUIDED

Creating High-Impact Products
in the Face of Uncertainty

EVIDENCE GUIDED

Creating High-Impact Products in the Face of Uncertainty

ITAMAR GILAD

Author and Illustrations: Itamar Gilad

Editor: Jonathan Norman

Cover Art: Jason Anscomb design

Interior Design: Susana Cardona

ISBN: 978-84-09-53639-9

Published by Itamar Gilad (itamargilad.com)

Contents

CHAPTER 7

Scaling GIST. 143

CHAPTER 8

GIST Patterns. 161

CHAPTER 9

Adopting GIST 177

To my parents, Giora and Yaffa Gilad

Introduction:
Why Evidence-Guided?

In my line of work, I regularly get to hear product people and managers explain what they plan to do with their products—strategies, roadmaps, new products, and features. I'm always impressed by the thought and creativity that goes into these. However, at the end of the presentation I'm often left wanting.

Then I ask the question that's on my mind:

How do you know that these are the right things to do?

This may sound like a silly thing to ask, but I'm not trying to be cute. The answers are meaningful, and can be divided into two groups. There are those who don't find the question surprising at all, and can readily share research, test results, and learnings in support of their ideas. The second, and more common reaction, is one of silent bewilderment. What do I mean "how do you *know*?" The plan was conceived, reviewed, and approved by smart and experienced people. Often it is derived from some bigger plan, and is backed by irrefutable logic or impressive-sounding data ("we pitched the feature to six customers and they all liked it"). These responses represent two drastically different schools of product development. The former is typical of companies making use of *evidence* to form decisions, while the latter, unbeknownst to them, are companies that heavily rely on *opinions*.

Having used both approaches myself for 20 years as a product manager and developer, and having consulted many product companies since, I can tell you there's a world of difference between evidence-guided development, and opinion-based development; not just in the way you plan and execute, but in the results you see. Evidence-guided companies understand there's a lot of uncertainty in the game and are tilting the odds in their favor. Opinion-based companies are effectively placing blind bets on a roulette table. You may get rich both ways, but one works much more consistently.

Evidence-guided development is not about ceding decisions to data; it's about supercharging our judgment and helping us make better decisions. It's also not slower—it's much faster. Done right, evidence-guided approaches improve resource efficiency, reduce planning time, suppress politics, build trust, empower people and teams, and, most importantly, deliver value to the business and to the customers faster. It's the way any truly successful product company you know is operating (or has operated in its best days).

Test Yourself

Are you working for an evidence-guided company? If you're unsure, try filling out the scorecard below.

Go ahead, it will only take a minute.

GIST Scorecard

For each item below enter a score of 0%–100% showing how much you're practicing this element of the system. Then you can average the scores in each category—goals, ideas, steps, tasks—and average again across categories to get your final score.

- **Goals**

  - We identified what impact (value delivered and value captured) means for us and are measuring impact using a very small set of top-level metrics ____%

  - We mapped out multiple levels of submetrics that contribute to our top metrics, and know how they are interconnected ____%

  - All goals are expressed in terms of outcomes (measurable improvements) and not output (things we will do) ____%

— All teams have team-level goals which they define _____%

— Goals are well aligned top-down, bottom-up, and across _____%

Goals average score _____%

- **Ideas**

  — We're constantly collecting ideas and are willing to evaluate any idea no matter where it comes from _____%

  — Each team manages its own list of ideas that is open for anyone to see _____%

  — We pick ideas on the basis of their impact, ease, and supporting evidence (confidence) _____%

  Ideas average score _____%

- **Steps**

  — All ideas are validated through at least one form of test, experiment, or release test before fully launching _____%

  — We re-evaluate ideas based on test results _____%

  — Ideas that don't produce supporting evidence are modified or parked _____%

  Steps average _____%

- **Tasks**

  — Team members are involved in defining goals, ideas, and validation steps _____%

  — All teams regularly and frequently review the status of goals, ideas, and steps and update them as necessary _____%

  — All tasks (sprint items or Kanban cards) are clearly associated with one or more discovery or delivery steps _____%

  Tasks average score _____%

Total score: _____% [average across Goals, Ideas, Steps, and Tasks]

No one gets a perfect score in this test, but if filling the scorecard made you realize you have room to improve, this book may be right for you.

The scorecard is arranged according to the *GIST model* that breaks the adoption of evidence-guided development into four concrete areas: *Goals, Ideas, Steps,* and *Tasks*. I'll teach you how to use GIST in depth in this book.

Who Is This Book For?

I wrote this book to help product people who wish to start working in an evidence-guided way—product managers, UX designers, and engineers at all levels up to CPO, CTO, and Head of Design.

If you're involved in product development as a UX researcher, data analyst, product marketing manager, agile coach, or other role, you may find a lot of value in learning how evidence-guided development works. I warn you that things can get pretty technical and detailed.

The models and processes described in this book are widely applicable. You'll find use for them whether you're developing for businesses, consumers, developers, or internal customers, and whether your company is a startup, a scale-up, or an enterprise.

How to Use This Book

If you're like me, you rarely read business management books from cover to cover. Here's a map to help guide you:

- Chapter 1 explains the GIST model and the reason for using it as demonstrated by two stories from my time at Google. I recommend you don't skip this chapter.

- Chapters 2–5 cover the four layers of the GIST model—Goals, Ideas, Steps, and Tasks—in detail. I explain the principles and models as well as a large number of practical techniques. If you're working in a product team, or are managing people working in such teams, I highly recommend reading these chapters. If you're a senior manager and are short on time, you may wish to jump directly to Chapter 6 to get an overview of the system, and then go back and read the parts you find most relevant.

- Chapters 6–8 deal with adapting the model to your type of company. Chapter 6, The Evidence-Guided Company, gives a full worked example of a midsize company using GIST, and explains the evidence-guided versions of product strategy, big projects, and roadmaps. Chapter 7, Scaling GIST, explains how GIST works in companies of various sizes—from startup to enterprise. Chapter 8, GIST Patterns, talks about GIST in B2B, B2C, Multi-sided marketplaces, Platforms and Services teams, and physical products. These chapters will be of most value for senior product people and for managers.

- Chapter 9, Adopting GIST, talks about the challenges and objections I commonly see when introducing evidence-guided development into companies, and ways to overcome them. This is an important chapter for anyone who's attempting to drive the change in their own team, group, business unit, or organization.

Companion Page—For all the information I included in this book, there's a lot more I couldn't include for the sake of brevity and readability. For this reason I have set up a *companion page* at EvidenceGuided.com/BookResources where you'll find eBooks, templates, links to articles, and further explanations. My aim is to keep this as an active, continually updated resource that reflects the latest learnings. As a reader of this book you get access to the page free of charge (signup may be required for some resources).

Courses—I also offer paid evidence-guided online courses (live and self-paced) to build up your knowledge and skills of the techniques listed in the book. See: EvidenceGuided.com/courses.

For many years I was solidly in the opinion-based camp. I thought I had product management figured out, and I trusted my intuition and my wits to lead me. But one major project at Google offered a rude awakening. This story is where the book begins.

CHAPTER I

From Opinions to Evidence

It was August 2011, and I had just joined Gmail as a product manager. As I reported for duty on my first day, my head was buzzing with ideas for how I might make my mark on Google's flagship email service, and, who knows, maybe even *reinvent email*. But of course it was not to be. Google had plans of its own for Gmail and there was already a big, strategic project waiting for me.

You've probably heard of Google+. Maybe you even used it at one point. In the early 2010s, with the threat of Facebook looming over its advertising business, Google decided to go all-in on Social. Google+ wasn't just a new social network, built from the ground up with all the bells and whistles, it was an entirely new division within Google and the cornerstone of its strategy. Bradley Horowitz, the Vice President of products for Google+, explained this strategy in a 2011 interview: "Google+ is Google itself. We're extending it across all that we do— search, ads, Chrome, Android, Maps, YouTube—so that each of those services contributes to our understanding of who you are."[1]

And that's where we, Gmail, came in. Our mission was to connect Gmail and Google+ and make them feel as a part of one whole. This seemed like a reasonable and important thing to do. Social networks were growing at a pace never seen before, and people were spending hours each day using them. Early Google+ was growing fast too. By October 2011, just months after its launch, it already had 40 million users. Three months later, it officially had 90 million. These were small numbers compared to Facebook's 800 million active users, but it was a promising start that made us quietly optimistic.

So, off we went. We brainstormed, designed, and built features that brought elements of Google+ into Gmail: you could share photos from Gmail to Google+, see the latest posts from your friends in a side panel next to your inbox, and filter messages by Circles (Google+ friend groups). These were not necessarily cheap or easy projects to pull off. Some carried on until late 2013. Other product ideas were put on hold to allow the Google+ projects to jump to the head of the queue.

This story ends in a sadly familiar way. A small group of enthusiasts adopted the Google+ features in Gmail and loved them, but most other users just disregarded our hard work, and some clearly disliked the mix of social and personal. We persevered and continued to launch according to plan, but the results we hoped for never came. Eventually, after years of low usage, we discontinued all the Google+ features. Today, you won't find them in Gmail.

Google+ itself didn't fare much better. While user numbers grew strongly on paper, only a small subset of users remained truly active and engaged. It seemed that most people just didn't need another social network. The Google+ team iterated and launched new features and redesigns at a fast pace, but to no avail. Google+ didn't become an important part of most Google users' lives, Facebook continued to grow as before, as did Google's ad business. Eventually, after years of hard work, it became clear that Google's social strategy had failed and the project lost momentum. Parts of Google+ were spun off into separate products, and the core social network was shut down in 2019.

But the bad news didn't end there. With the benefit of hindsight we now know that by placing all its bets on Google+, Google had missed a much larger opportunity presented by social mobile apps such as WhatsApp, Instagram, and Snapchat. These apps eventually became the threat to Facebook that Google+ aspired to be, and they did it at a fraction of the cost and effort.

Opinion-Based Development

With Google+, Google followed a classic product development pattern— we picked a promising idea, turned it into a plan, then switched to execution. Google+ was a big, strategic idea (which made its failure all the more obvious), but I see companies use this same *plan-and-execute* approach for anything from minor product enhancements to major new features and products. With plan-and-execute we have to start by picking which ideas to invest in. The decision usually involves some data—a customer request, what the leading competitor is doing, the latest trend in the market—but is mostly based on our own *judgment*. We rely on our experience and logic to form opinions, and on consensus and rank to arrive at decisions. Many companies repeat the plan-and-execute process at multiple nested levels: strategy, roadmap, product, and feature, creating what I call a *Planning Waterfall*.

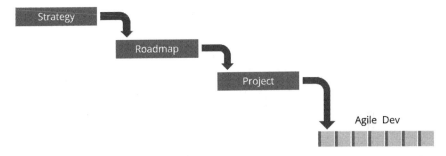

FIGURE 1.1: The Planning Waterfall

Human judgment is extremely powerful, but it can also be very flawed. While for most day-to-day decisions experience, logic, and consensus are perfectly adequate, psychologists have found that we struggle with questions that entail complexity, uncertainty, and too little or too much information.[2] For example, when we debate a question like "which of these 12 ideas is the most likely to achieve the goal?" we have to consider the users, the market, the product, the technology, as well as the internal dynamics of our company. These are all complex things, full of moving parts, and in constant change. Many ideas, including ones that seem like sure bets, will fail to make an impact, or produce unexpected side effects. Our brains, powerful as they are, are simply not able to compute all the probabilities and arrive at a correct decision.

But instead of telling us "I don't know" our brains use a trick: they fall back to *cognitive biases* such as *confirmation bias, risk aversion,* the *sunk cost fallacy,* and hundreds more.[3] Our cognitive biases can not only lead us to the wrong decision, but they can also make us feel overly confident in this decision (and perhaps make us believe it's the only one possible). Debating ideas in groups or committees doesn't fix the problem, as groups introduce their own biases such as groupthink and politics. Trusting experienced and senior people to choose has been shown time and again to be unreliable (the leadership team of Google had some of the smartest, most successful executives in the industry). The result is plans that are full of questionable decisions and bad ideas.

All of this may sound overly pessimistic to you. Product companies are obviously capable of making good decisions; the results are all around us. But that may just be survivorship bias. We see the successes, but below the surface there's an awful lot of hidden failure. If you analyze usage in your product you're likely to see that most features get little or no traction with users.[4] You can remove them today and almost no one will notice. Product portfolios have a similar power law: a few products generate all the traction and revenue, while others contribute very little. Research of thousands of A/B experiments across multiple companies shows that at most one in three product ideas show measurable improvement,[5] and the average in the industry may be far lower. If these numbers are true for you, then the majority of what's currently in your roadmap and product backlog isn't worth doing; it will just create waste at high cost.

Evidence-Guided Development

Some companies seem to defy the odds and produce hit after hit over the course of years and decades. Google is one of those companies. For me that was a key reason to join; frustrated with my own track record of success I wanted to understand what made Google different. What I discovered was that Google didn't find a way to predict the future, but rather created a system that acknowledged uncertainty and worked to improve the ratio of success versus failure. With Google+ Google obviously used a different playbook (perhaps because of the existential threat that Facebook presented), but historically the company always started with customer-focused goals (internal principle: *Start with the user and all else will follow*); it was willing to try out many ideas to address these goals (*Let a thousand flowers bloom*), and wasn't shy about testing minimal, unpolished products with users (*Think big, but start small*). Perhaps most important, Google expected its product teams to act on the results, even if that meant pivoting or shutting down the project (*Fail fast*). Underlying all of this was a strong emphasis on data, both quantitative and qualitative.

Google is not unique in this approach. One of Amazon's principles is "We go where the data leads us." Airbnb, Netflix, Microsoft, Slack, Booking.com, Facebook/Meta, Apple, and many successful but lesser-known companies, all have their own variation of this same theme. The processes these companies employ are very different, but they have one thing in common: they supercharge human judgment with *evidence*.

Evidence is facts and information that confirm or refute our assumptions and theories (different from *data*, which is simply facts and information, but not necessarily with any meaning). Using evidence helps us break away from our internal perceptions and biases. It forces us to confront reality and to update our picture of the world. For this reason evidence is a foundational element of science, medicine, and law; disciplines where it's recognized that decisions should not be made solely on the basis of human judgment. *Evidence-guided development* attempts to bring these same concepts to the creation of products. It's a key part of all modern development methodologies including Lean Startup, Design Thinking, Product Discovery, and Growth.

The GIST Model

While at Google I had a chance to experience evidence-guided development firsthand (a full example is coming shortly). It was a real revelation—a completely different way to develop products. In 2017 I left Google and started consulting product organizations, eager to share what I learned. But I then realized there was yet a bigger problem. Most of the people I talked with already knew the concepts, but few were able to implement them in their companies. Evidence-guided development goes against the grain of long-held "best practices" and requires rethinking company power dynamics. It's hard to get managers and stakeholders to give up on release roadmaps, and it's equally hard to convince product teams that their job is to discover as well as deliver.

At Google I observed that it's useful to break evidence-guided development into four areas of change: goal-setting, idea selection, experimentation, and execution. To make it easier for my clients to tackle these changes one at a time I created a four-layer model I called *GIST: Goals, Ideas, Steps, and Tasks.*

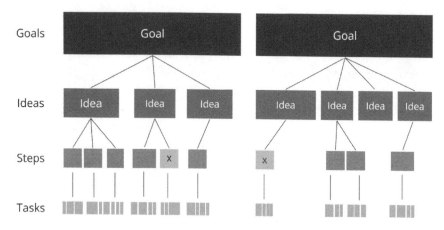

FIGURE 1.2: An example of the GIST model at work. The team is considering a total of seven *ideas* across two *goals*. It is using *steps* to develop and test the ideas, and each step breaks into *tasks*. Some ideas fail during testing (marked with x in the diagram) and are dropped, making room for work on other ideas.

Goals define the outcomes we wish to achieve—measurable benefits for customers and for the business. *Ideas* are hypothetical ways to achieve the goals. The key word here is hypothetical. As most ideas don't work, we have to test multiple ideas and invest only in those that yield supporting evidence. That's the job of *Steps*: short projects or activities that develop an idea somewhat (often with no coding) *and* test it. A step may be as simple as creating a model on paper, or as complex as a beta launch. *Tasks* are the work items that go into doing the work—the things we manage using Scrum, Kanban, or other methods. GIST doesn't dictate how you manage tasks, but it strives to connect the work to steps, ideas, and goals, allowing the team to work with full context and deep focus on the customers and the business. The GIST framework applies to small, medium, and large product ideas. It can be used in a ten-person startup as well as in a 10,000-person enterprise.

GIST is not a radically new concept. I consider it a meta-framework that combines tried-and-tested product methodologies with models and tools I created along the way. Still, when I started sharing GIST the reaction from the product community and from my clients was overwhelmingly positive. There seemed to be a strong need for a practical framework that "puts it all together." Many people were willing to give GIST a go, and the information they shared helped me iterate, improve, and create the framework described in this book. Still, it's important not to consider GIST a fixed process. It's a model that helps bring evidence-guided thinking into your development, but you should test it and adapt to your context.

To make things less theoretical, let me tell you about the first project in which I experienced the power of evidence-guided development—my proto-GIST project at Gmail.

The Tabbed Inbox

In late 2011, not long after we shipped the first wave of Google+ integrations, I had an idea. I noticed that my personal inbox (Gmail, of course) was full of promotions, social updates, and notifications that I didn't care to read, but had too little time or motivation to delete. In Gmail, we called this situation *inbox clutter*. Wouldn't it be cool, I thought, if Gmail just magically organized my inbox, without me having to do any work? I imagined the non-important email showing as a digest in a side panel: "You also received 5 promotions, 12 social messages, and 3 receipts." Users would be able to click on the digest and read these less important messages when the mood strikes them.

As is often the case, I fell in love with my own idea and immediately wanted to push it forward for funding, planning, and execution. But my managers and colleagues were not convinced, and they had their reasons. It wasn't clear that inbox clutter was indeed a widespread and severe problem among casual users, who on average received very little mail. Gmail already had multiple features to help manage your inbox, but none got a lot of usage. Worse, my idea to push low-priority mail to the side could easily confuse and annoy the users who were used to having their inbox work in a certain way ever since Gmail launched in 2004.

My colleagues and managers were pushing back on my idea, but implicitly they were asking me some very Googly questions: What are you trying to achieve? Who is this for? What would be considered a success? In other words, *what is the goal?*

At that time Gmail had a product-wide goal to become more relevant and engaging in a world increasingly dominated by social networks and instant messaging. I argued that solving inbox clutter is how we, the Gmail Inbox team, could contribute to this broader goal. My team, skeptical as it was, was willing to explore. We started with research to understand inbox clutter better. One of our backend developers ran a large data analysis to see how consumer users process their inboxes. The data he brought back took us by surprise. A huge portion of Gmail's users did not manage their inbox in any way. They just went through their emails and read selected messages, otherwise leaving everything they received untouched.

What does such an inbox look like? We got the answer when we interviewed casual Gmail users and asked them to show us their inboxes. We realized that average statistics didn't tell the whole story. With the proliferation of social networks and eCommerce, these people got substantial amounts of promotions, social notifications, and transactional emails. Some had tens of thousands of unread messages in their inbox. They had to work hard to spot important new messages, and even harder to get back to those messages later. Inbox clutter was a much bigger problem than we thought.

Armed with this information, we were able to formulate an objective: help casual users interact only with the messages they want to interact with. This entailed a few success metrics: being able to accurately predict which messages users wish to read; ensuring that they would never miss out on an important message, and most importantly, high levels of user engagement and satisfaction with the new experience as measured by usage, retention, and surveys. This goal served us in the months to come: we knew who we were focusing on and what success looks like.

Now it was time to discuss ideas. We had a few: teaching users how to clean their inbox themselves, grouping or reordering inbox messages in various ways, and creating digests of the least important messages (my initial idea). Each idea had its pros and cons, and different people had their favorite. However, debating the ideas didn't lead to any useful conclusion. We knew we had to test, and we had to start with the riskiest part: the user experience.

So we brought people into our usability lab to test some of these ideas. In one of those tests, we asked 12 participants to use Gmail, but with a difference—the inbox was split into tabs. The main tab contained mail from friends and family, but there were other tabs for social notifications, promotions, and transactions. When opening each tab, the participants found their very own messages, taken from their inbox, sorted into the right place. As if by magic, Gmail organized their inbox by mail category.

This part of the study was a complete sham of course. The thing the participants saw wasn't Gmail, but a thin facade of HTML that our user experience designers cooked up. You could do little with it except look at your inbox and click into the tabs. Message categorization was another bit of sleight of hand. With the participants' permission, and while they were being interviewed, a few of us sat in a separate room and copied the first 50 messages from their inbox—sender and subject only—into the appropriate tab, based on our own best guesses. It was a bit of a race against time, but it worked. The participants experienced the Tabbed Inbox (almost) as if it was a real thing.

The results? All the participants immediately understood what was going on and could explain why the messages were placed where they were. Using the tabs was natural and easy. Best of all, 10 of the 12 participants absolutely loved this new inbox. In fact, many of them asked how soon they could have it. The smiles on their faces told a clear story—this was something they needed, but never knew they could have. The other two participants already had their inbox under control using other Gmail functions, so they didn't find the new inbox appealing. Interestingly this same ratio of 10–15 percent of people who already managed their personal inboxes well and thought that the Tabbed Inbox was unnecessary, repeated throughout our research over the next 14 months. Unfortunately, this minority included many of my colleagues at Gmail, and as we discovered later, most of the tech press.

Given these strong results we decided to double-down on the Tabbed Inbox idea and leave other ideas as fallbacks. Still, we didn't go all-in. Our initial research gave us sufficient evidence just to fund a small project—a rudimentary, functioning version of the inbox with a bare-bones user interface and simplistic classification. We used this early version to self-test on our own personal inboxes (in Gmail this is called *Fishfood*—team testing). I remember having to convince my team members to stop diligently organizing their inboxes and to let email pile up, just like ordinary users. It was an adjustment for some, but we quickly realized that even with this basic version of the inbox, the experience was quite transformative.

Throughout the project, we kept progressing in stepwise increments—build a more-evolved version of the inbox, then test it. Along the way, we enlisted the help of thousands of Googlers who valiantly agreed to use an interim version of the inbox in their own personal accounts (this process is commonly called *Dogfooding*). We exposed our evolving email classification system to a small subset of Gmail users through a lab (an optional feature you can enable in Settings) where they could report classification mistakes. This gave us much-needed data to improve our algorithms. We continued to perform regular external user studies as well, some involving hundreds of participants using the new inbox over periods of weeks.

The project definitely didn't go according to any plan. We had to redesign the user interface multiple times, and getting the classification right required assembling a small team of data and machine-learning specialists. We also learned that launching the new inbox on the desktop version of Gmail first, per the plan, was not enough—inbox clutter was an even bigger problem on mobile where it was causing excessive notifications. So we expanded the project to include the Android and iOS Gmail apps. I didn't have to pitch very hard to get these other teams to join the project; the evidence we collected did the talking for me.

The new inbox was launched in May 2013 to generally lukewarm reviews from the tech press, but we didn't really care. By then, we had tested the new feature with thousands of users and were fairly certain we had found a winner. Still, the testing continued. We gradually switched more and more accounts into the new experience (programatically skipping those 10–15 percent who looked like they had things under control) and tracked their behavior, satisfaction levels, and classification error rates.

The rollout was uneventful, with very little backlash and tons of positive feedback. People loved the fact that social and marketing emails no longer competed with emails from friends and family, and never buzzed their phones. It was easy to switch off the new feature, but few users did, and our data confirmed they were using the inbox as we expected. The Tabbed Inbox won a number of innovation awards inside Google, and was generally recognized as one of the most important improvements to the product. It was a fun project to work on, and, more importantly, one that created high impact. Today, the Tabbed Inbox is the first thing the majority of Gmail's users see, and we have strong evidence to show it's giving them lots of value.

The Elements of GIST

The story of the Tabbed Inbox brings together many of the elements of the GIST model. Let's look at it again from the perspective of goals, ideas, steps, and tasks.

Goals

I tried to kick off the project around an idea. Had I succeeded, the implicit goal would have been "let's launch Itamar's new inbox," which would have been great for my ego, but not so much for the end results. Such goals, often called *output goals*, are very common in the industry and very harmful. When most ideas yield little or no value, betting on an unproven idea is likely to produce waste. Luckily in this case I was forced to backtrack and form an *outcome goal* centered on *measurably* improving the inbox experience of casual Gmail users. This goal helped focus us on the destination rather than on the way.

In Chapter 2, Goals, I'll show you how to lead your area of responsibility, whether it's a company, business unit, group, or team, with a concise set of outcome goals. We will see how to pick goals using the North Star Metric and metrics trees and express them in the popular format of Objectives and Key Results (OKR). Then we'll talk about how leaders can steer without deciding what to work on, and how to tackle the tough challenge of aligning the goals top-down, bottom-up, and across the organization.

Ideas

Once we, the Gmail Inbox team, had a goal in place, we were ready to discuss ideas. But instead of trying to pick the winning idea through brainstorms, debate, and reviews, we did three common-sense things that are not at all common: 1) we based our ideas on research rather than opinions, 2) we evaluated which ideas seem most promising given the data we had, and 3) we went on to test multiple ideas.

This process is at the heart of GIST. In Chapter 3, Ideas, I'll show you how to collect ideas in idea banks, and how to evaluate and compare them in a fast, objective, and unbiased way. A key component of this evaluation is *Confidence*, which measures the strength of the evidence in support of an idea. I'll teach you how to use the Confidence Meter (see Figure 1.3), a tool I created specifically for this purpose and that today is used by numerous companies, including Google. We'll see how to cut prioritization debates short and how to leave politics and pressure tactics out of the discussion.

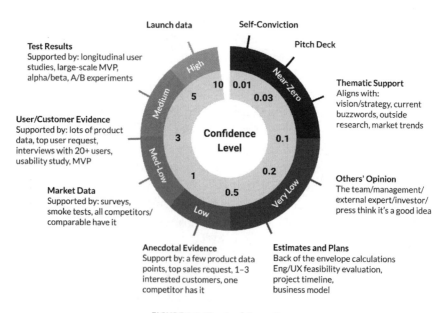

FIGURE 1.3: The Confidence Meter

What about Opportunities?

Many people find it helpful to connect ideas to what is now known as *opportunities* (formerly called *customer problems*, or *underserved user needs*). If that describes your approach, you can certainly use it with GIST. If you uncover an important user need you can turn addressing it into a goal (as we did for Inbox Clutter in the Tabbed Inbox project) or you can use it as a filter for the type of ideas you'd like to pursue. You can also keep a list or a tree[6] of opportunities alongside the artifacts of GIST. In Chapter 6 we will talk about *strategic opportunities*, which is a related but different concept to do with strategy formation.

Steps

In the Tabbed Inbox project we were lucky to land on a strong idea relatively early in our product discovery. But many initially promising ideas turn out to be duds, and even the good ones need iteration and refinement. For this reason we built the Tabbed Inbox through a series of build-measure-learn loops, which are called *Steps* in GIST. There were usability tests, longitudinal studies, fishfood and dogfood, labs, and partial launches. Each step generated a more complete version of the product, but also gave us new evidence, which helped build our confidence in the idea and get more funding. We used what we learned in each step to course-correct and improve the idea. The feature we eventually launched was profoundly better than the one we started with.

Many product organizations I meet are familiar with this important concept, which Product Management guru Marty Cagan has aptly named, *Product Discovery*, but struggle to implement it—they build too much and test too little; even when they do test they fail to learn and take meaningful action. In Chapter 4, Steps, I'll walk you through a full example of how to take a high-potential idea, and get it through a series of steps to a clear Yes/No decision that no person, no matter how opinionated, will dispute. This process isn't meant just for big ideas; cheap ideas entail risks too and should similarly be validated, although faster and with fewer steps. In Chapter 4, we will review the wide gamut of validation techniques at our disposal—from data analysis through smoke tests to A/B experiments—and how to combine them into a development project.

Tasks

You might have noticed in my story how involved my product team was in shaping the product. That is a norm in many good product companies, but not a very common practice in the industry. There's a double problem: the managers don't trust the team to make good decisions, and team members are increasingly focused on delivery and seem disinterested in business and user goals. Even in companies where these are not major issues, teams struggle to reconcile product discovery with their agile development practices.

Working with strong people is one of the benefits of joining Google, but that's not the only reason my team was so engaged. Google was able to create an environment that allowed rank-and-file employees to be in the know, to contribute, and to make decisions. In Chapter 5, Tasks, we'll talk about how to do the same with your team, by involving them in all four layers of the GIST stack, and by having them own discovery as well as delivery. I'll also share a tool—the GIST board—to help jointly manage the work of the team across goals, ideas, and steps.

Driving the Change

There's nothing particularly revolutionary about GIST, and it's not the only evidence-guided model out there. Many good product companies have been working in similar ways for years, although they probably don't call what they do GIST. Still, I see far more companies that try to incorporate evidence into their work, but get stuck halfway between the old model and the new. These companies adopt new processes, but get few benefits. Part of the problem is overcoming entrenched mindsets and practices. In order to move forward you need to change the way your managers, stakeholders, and team think and behave.

The second half of the book is devoted to helping you adopt evidence-guided development in your organization. In Chapter 6, The Evidence-Guided Company, we'll see how evidence-guided thinking can be deployed across an entire company, and what role managers, stakeholders, and product teams play in this brave new world. We'll also talk about the often-sticky topics of product strategy, big projects, cross-team dependencies, and roadmaps. In Chapter 7, Scaling GIST, I'll show you how evidence-guided development works in startups, in midsize companies, and in enterprises. Chapter 8, GIST Patterns, talks about GIST in common types of products and business models: B2B, B2C, physical products, marketplaces, and internal platforms and services. Chapter 9, Adopting GIST, discusses ways to smooth the adoption curve and to deal with common objections.

How big of a transformation you're facing depends on where you are today. GIST may not work in a very traditional organization where decisions strictly flow top-down, and where the function of the product org is merely "delivery." However, if your company isn't that extreme (most aren't) there's a good chance you can adopt GIST, and it's even likely that your colleagues will be in support. I regularly teach GIST to product leads, engineers, executives, and business folk, and once the model is clear, the response is almost always "we need this" and "let's do it!"

At the end of the day, meaningful change is never easy or comfortable; it takes visionary, motivated, and persistent people to push it forward. If you're a product manager tired of building things that nobody needs, a manager frustrated with the rate of innovation in your organization, or an engineer or designer that feels that most of what you create is a waste, GIST was created to help *you* drive the change in your own organization. It's not going to be an overnight switch, but I can guarantee you that it'll be a worthwhile journey.

Let's get started.

Takeaways

- The classic approach of plan-and-execute forces us to commit to a plan while facing high levels of uncertainty.
- Our brains and our decision processes are not well suited to making decisions when confronted with uncertainty. We rely on opinions, sparse data, consensus, and rank, backed by cognitive biases, group dynamics, and politics.
- The track record of success in the industry is abysmal. Research indicates that only a minority of ideas create measurable impact, and a high ratio of launched features and products get little or no use.
- Evidence-guided companies improve the odds of success by supercharging human judgment with evidence. They continuously evaluate and test ideas and update the plans based on what they learn.
- The principles of guiding our decisions by evidence are not new, but they are hard for companies to adopt as they go against traditional best practices and corporate power dynamics.
- I created the GIST model—Goals, Ideas, Steps, Tasks—to help break the change into four distinct areas: goal-setting, idea evaluation, experimentation, and execution.

- The Tabbed Inbox story, while not perfect (no project is), is an example of the GIST model in action. Starting with user/business-centered goals. Considering multiple ideas, iterating by running the ideas through various steps, each producing a more complete version of the feature and more supporting evidence. Optimizing the work for both discovery and delivery.

- The first chapters of the book are devoted to explaining the GIST model in detail. Chapter 6 covers a full-company example. Chapters 7 and 8 describe how to adapt the model to the size and type of company you work in. And Chapter 9 explains how to tackle objections, and smooth the adoption curve.

Notes

[1] "Inside Google Plus | WIRED." Sep. 27, 2011, https://www.wired.com/2011/09/ff-google-horowitz/. Accessed Aug. 21, 2020.

[2] The book *Thinking Fast and Slow* by Nobel-winning psychologist Daniel Kahneman explains this phenomenon in detail.

[3] For a full list of cognitive biases see: https://en.wikipedia.org/wiki/List_of_cognitive_biases

[4] A 2019 research conducted by Pendo.io suggests that 80% of features are rarely or never used. https://www.pendo.io/resources/the-2019-feature-adoption-report

[5] Kohavi, Ron, Diane Tang, and Ya Xu. 2020. *Trustworthy Online Controlled Experiments: A Practical Guide to A/B Testing*. Cambridge University Press. https://experimentguide.com/ Chapter 1.

[6] As described by Teresa Torres in her book *Continuous Discovery Habits*.

CHAPTER 2
Goals

Many product companies I meet practice a cyclical planning ritual. At the end of every quarter busy people across the organization lock themselves for days and weeks in meeting rooms (physical or virtual) to discuss what they should work on in the following quarter. No one seems to love these planning sessions, and the resulting plan is rarely followed to the letter, but the planning process seems imperative. At the end of the year there's yearly planning, which is much the same, just worse.

Observing the planning sessions reveals an interesting fact: the people in the room are debating ideas—what should we do—without first agreeing on the goals—what should we achieve. This often leads to strong misalignment. Some people care about short-term revenue, while others about the success of the strategy. One participant may consider product quality the top priority, while for another user experience is the most important thing. In this void of goals it's hard to come to an agreement as every idea may seem important to someone. Decisions are made on the basis of negotiation, compromise, or the opinion of the most senior person in the room. After the fact, some people are left dissatisfied and distrusting of the plan. Still, once the plan is in place, executing it becomes the goal.

Evidence-guided companies take a very different approach to planning. They define firm, measurable goals that state what positive changes they wish to create, known as *outcomes*, but adapt their plans on the go as new information emerges. They empower the people doing the work to discover the best way to achieve the goals, and to say no to requests that pull away from them. This form of leadership may feel unnatural and risky at first, but it is extremely powerful in the face of uncertainty. That's why the first layer of the GIST model is all about goals.

Evidence-Guided Goals

In the early 1970s, and while still very much an upstart, Intel found itself at the epicenter of a massive semiconductor revolution that would change the world. The opportunities ahead were immense, but so were the challenges and risks. Intel's forward-thinking CEO, Andy Grove, knew that to survive and thrive the company would have to move fast, respond quickly to new information, and yet maintain extreme focus and alignment. Ever an innovator, he adopted the relatively novel leadership approach of *Management by Objectives and Self Control* (MBO) proposed by management thinker Peter Drucker. According to MBO an organization and all its parts have to direct themselves toward *objectives* (what we now call *goals*), which Drucker compared to the destination of a ship at sea. Drucker argued that people and teams should participate in setting the objectives and be allowed to find their own way to achieve them—the often-forgotten principle of self-control.

A scientist by training, Grove determined that to be effective, goals have to be made measurable, removing any ambiguity about what's expected and whether the goal was accomplished. He invented a new way to express goals that he called (you guessed it): *Objectives and Key Results (OKR)*. In the following years Intel trained all its managers and employees in the use of OKR, and by all accounts the methodology was key to Intel's success, including during a risky full-company pivot onto microprocessors in the 1980s. Fifty years later, Objective and Key Results is still going strong as a method to express and manage goals. Google, Dropbox, Amazon, and many others practice it religiously and it has spread well beyond the tech industry.

OKR is not a mandatory part of GIST, but because it's so popular I'll use it to show goals throughout the book. You're probably already familiar with the format, but I'm including below a quick refresher, which may include some less-known things. For a deeper explanation of the methodology, you'll find a complimentary eBook on the companion page of this book.

An OKR expresses a goal in three parts:

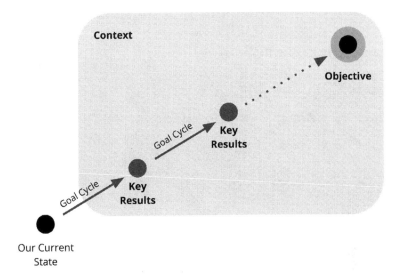

FIGURE 2.1: Objective and Key Results goal parts

- Objective—A short statement that describes the desired end state or the direction of change, for example: *Independent content creators can find an audience and monetize their work.* Objectives are supposed to be aspirational and inspiring, but not necessarily measurable or even fully feasible.
- Key results—2–5 measurable targets that define what success is in the current goal cycle. The best key results define both the current value and the target, for example: *Grow the ratio of content creators with more than 10,000 followers from 8.5% to 10%.*
- Context (optional)—This is not a part of the original Intel OKR structure, but I find it very helpful. The context is a short explanation as to why you think this goal is important, what relevant evidence you've found, and what other information you think will help the person working on the goal. The context can be embedded into the OKR, or placed in a separate document.

OKRs are set in cycles, typically a year for a company and a quarter everywhere else (startups sometimes use shorter cycles). While the objective may stay constant, we will adjust the key results from cycle to cycle. During the cycle we need to revisit the OKRs repeatedly to assess our progress and sometimes to adjust the goals.

Here's an example: the quarterly OKR of a product team responsible for customer onboarding—the process of getting a new customer to install the product, set it up, and start using it.

- O: All customers onboard quickly and successfully
  - KR1: Reduce average onboarding time from 30 days to 4 days
    // Why: Many potential customers end the trial period before they fully onboard
  - KR2: Increase onboarding completion rate from 72% to 80%

Note how the OKR paints a clear picture of what the team is trying to achieve in the long term (the objective) and during this quarter, but not how it'll do it. This is how it should be. Agreeing with managers and stakeholders about what positive change, or outcomes, the team should deliver is an important discussion we should hold every quarter. Attempting to decide which product ideas are best is likely to be a waste of everyone's time. Worse, if these ideas are baked into the OKRs (as many teams do, sometimes under a redundant "Initiatives" section), the team will be motivated to focus on *output*—delivering on the plan—rather than on the outcomes.

Choosing the Most Important Outcomes

Focusing the goals on outcomes rather than outputs is by now a well-understood principle, but one that is not easy to implement. Some companies struggle to identify any metrics other than revenue, market share, and maybe Net Promoter Score. Others try to cram every possible metric and key performance indicator into the OKRs, which only serves to hurt focus, completion rates, and trust in the goal system.

Evidence-guided companies derive outcomes and priorities from *models*. There are many good ways to model the behavior of your business and of your customers, for example funnels, flywheels, and user journeys.[1] I'll show you one model that is generally applicable to any type of organization.

The Value Exchange Loop

At its core, every organization aims to do two things: deliver value to its target market—users, customers, and partners—and capture value back. Delivering value means addressing the needs of your customers at a reasonable cost. Capturing value means getting the things you need to operate and grow, whether they are revenue, market share, or anything else. This principle of give-and-take is true for startups, scale-ups, corporations, government agencies, NGOs, internal platforms and services divisions, open-source communities, and any other type of organization you can think of. We all work in the service of someone else, and we all want to get something in return.

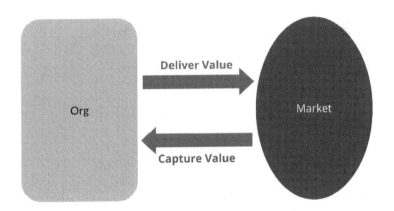

FIGURE 2.2: The value exchange loop

Success comes from tying value delivery and value capture in a virtuous loop. The more we give, the more the market will be willing to pay us back in revenue, market share, word-of-mouth, data, or attention. The more value we capture the more resources we have to scale the organization, improve our products and services, and deliver yet more value to more customers and users.

To ensure that our value exchange loop is working, we have to make it measurable. For this we can use two top-level metrics:

- The *North Star Metric* measures how much value we deliver

- The *Top Business Metric* measures how much value we capture

Let's start with the Top Business Metric as it is easier to understand. Your company is probably already measuring dozens of business metrics such as revenue, net income, number of paying customers, and monthly active users. These are all important, and we'd like to improve them all. However, trying to grow multiple aspects of the business at once is very hard and often counterproductive. It's good practice to choose one Top Business Metric that is (right now) the most important. For growth-focused companies the Top Business Metric is usually the number of active users or active customers (Amazon famously sacrificed profits for decades in favor of market growth). Companies seeking investment or an IPO may need to hit a certain revenue or profit target. Saying "This year we want to reach total revenue of €15M" doesn't mean that we don't care about profit or market share, but it does help people understand what's *most* important and make good tradeoffs.

Choosing a Top Business Metric is a strategic decision, and perhaps one you don't control. That's ok, you can still use GIST without it. You will, however, need a way to measure how much value you deliver.

The North Star Metric

Delivering high value to your market is not just a matter of altruism; it's genuinely the best thing you can do for your business. It's far easier to acquire and retain customers with high-value products, you can charge more for them, and they keep competitors at bay. Many modern product companies understand this and consider growing value-to-customer their most important goal. That's where the North Star Metric comes in.

A North Star Metric (NSM) is a number that sums up the core value we deliver to the market. In the words of growth expert Sean Ellis, it's your *value footprint*. Here are a few examples:

- **WhatsApp**—Messages sent per month
- **YouTube**—Minutes watched per month
- **eBay**—Gross merchandise value (GMV) per quarter
- **Airbnb**—Nights booked per month
- **HubSpot**—Weekly active teams
- **Amplitude**—Weekly learning users (WLU)

WhatsApp users come for free, rich messaging. Each message sent is therefore an increment of value. If the total number of messages sent is growing, this is most likely a positive sign that the company is helping more users communicate. YouTube viewers are looking for interesting or helpful videos to watch, and YouTube creators are seeking an audience to view their content. The number of minutes watched indicates how well the platform is delivering on these expectations.

eBay and Airbnb are two-sided marketplaces, and their North Star Metrics are about connecting supply with demand and facilitating transactions. Airbnb measures these in terms of nights booked, while eBay looks at the total amount of money that changes hands. Note that neither metric favors the transactions that are most profitable for the company; that would mix delivered value and captured value. The North Star Metric is solely about the value the users are getting.

North Star Metrics are just as useful for business-to-business companies. HubSpot, a maker of cloud-based sales and marketing tools, measures the number of *Weekly Active Teams* (WAT)[2] its products serve, since marketing collaboration is how customers get the most value from HubSpot's products. Amplitude, a maker of data analytics tools for web and mobile apps, is measuring *Weekly Learning Users (WLUs)*—the count of weekly users that found something so useful in the data that they share it with at least two other people.[3] Business customers, like consumers, are not interested in the product per se, they're interested in satisfying their needs at a perceivably reasonable cost, and that's what these North Star Metrics measure.

Finding Your North Star Metric

To figure out what your North Star is, you should ask "Why are customers using my product? What is the core value they seek?". Focus on the product and market as they are now. It's ok to change your NSM later as your company grows and diversifies. Larger companies that have several business units with different missions should choose different North Star Metrics for each.

Here's what you need to look for in a North Star Metric:

- **As close as possible to the core value experience**—When I helped a large online supermarket find its North Star Metric, the obvious choice was *Items Sold*. That's a perfectly reasonable NSM because people indeed come to a supermarket to buy groceries. However, after some consideration, we changed it to *Items Obtained*—the real goal is not to buy groceries but to have them. This North Star Metric reflects the important aspects of successful home delivery and gift items. Then, after some more thinking, the management team came back with an even better North Star Metric: *Items Consumed*. Obtaining food items that end up in the garbage bin is of no value to the customer. The better mission is therefore to help customers obtain just those items that they're likely to use (the managers assured me they have a way of measuring this on average). Ultimately this makes good business sense: wouldn't you want to shop in a supermarket that cares for your needs at this level? Wouldn't you tell your friends and family they should buy there as well?

- **Aggregate number, not a rate or ratio**—We're looking for a number that will sum up the value across the entire market and potentially grow up-and-to-right over time. So, *Total number of documents created* is good, but *Percentage of active users that create documents* is not. The latter is an important supporting metric, but it doesn't reflect the total amount of value created. A company serving a thousand dedicated customers may have a better ratio than one serving tens of millions, but the latter is the one with the larger value footprint.

- **Simple and memorable**—No North Star Metric is perfect. Some messages sent via WhatsApp may be spam, some items purchased on eBay may not be fully satisfactory to the buyer. That's fine as long as the number is still generally indicative of total value. It's better to stay with an imperfect yet understandable and memorable metric, than to try to guide people with a complex formula.

The Most Important Goal

It's the quarterly all-hands meeting and the CEO is addressing the company. As usual, she starts by citing the company's mission. Mission Statements are the top objective of the organization. They communicate the core value we wish to create for our users and customers—the positive change we want to make in the world. A well-known example is Google's "Organize the world's information and make it universally accessible and useful." LinkedIn chose "To connect the world's professionals to make them more productive and successful." TED's mission is simply to "Spread ideas."

Mission Statements are important, but are often too abstract and high level to guide people's daily work. As many senior leaders discovered, simply repeating the mission is rarely sufficient to change people's behaviors.

However, imagine that in this case the CEO continues to present the mission as a yearly company goal:

- Objective: Help enterprise employees express themselves better with smart docs // Our mission
  - KR: Grow number of docs created per month from 100K to 250K (+150%) // Our NSM
  - KR: Grow yearly revenue from $1.1M to $2M (+81%) // Our Top Business Metric

    // Context: see this doc to learn why we chose these metrics and these targets

The CEO reminds everyone why the company chose these top metrics, and why the leadership team feels these numbers are ambitious, yet realistic. She then shows a graph showing the current trajectory of the North Star Metric and Top Business Metric, indicating both are likely to fall short if no improvements are made. The CEO concludes by saying: "If you're unsure that what you're working on is going to contribute to the North Star Metric or the Top Business Metric, please immediately talk to your manager."

You can imagine how the temperature changes in the room. Perhaps for the first time everyone understands what top management considers success (you'd be surprised in how many companies this is not the case). By painting a clear target the CEO is helping the organization focus and align around a shared target.

Having two top metrics is important. While product people tend to focus more on value delivery, and business people tend to optimize more for value capture, everyone should be made aware that the collective mission is to achieve both. Having just one top-level metric ("Our North Star is profit") would leave a large part of the mission unrepresented, and may create an overly sales-driven or overly tech-focused company.

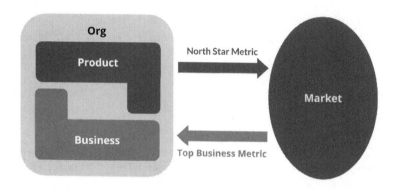

FIGURE 2.3: Having two top-level metrics reflects the dual mission

Metrics Trees

The North Star and Top Business Metrics are your most important measures of success, but they are affected by many factors and are slow to reflect changes (trailing indicators). It's therefore helpful to break them into submetrics (sometimes also called *input metrics)* which you can influence more readily.

In the example shown above the company chose *Number of Documents Created per Month* as its North Star Metric. One way to decompose this NSM would be:

Documents created per month =

   Number of monthly active users x Docs created per user per month

Even such a simple formula can give us useful insights. Do we have many active users, but few create more than one document? Perhaps the product is not delivering enough value to make it a daily or weekly habit. Do we have few active users, but each creates documents regularly? That may be good news; we may have found product/market fit and can now focus on acquiring more customers.

In a startup, the two submetrics can be assigned to individual teams, for example, the number of monthly active users may be the responsibility of the Growth team while growing the number of messages sent per user is handled by the Engagement team. This is a good way to define team ownership and mission, and to reduce dependencies. Naturally these teams can now set goals using their designated metrics, which essentially act as their *Local North Star*.

Pretty soon, though, both teams will discover that Monthly Active users and Documents Created per User are also hard to influence directly and should be further broken down. Another layer of supporting submetrics can be unearthed, and after it yet others. The question to ask at each level is "what changes in human or system behavior can cause the desired outcome?" If we continue down this path, we will end up with a metrics hierarchy, or tree, where every layer is more specific than the previous one (see Figure 2.4). At the leaves of the tree you may find exotic metrics such as *% of users that share a doc through chat* or *Number of PDFs converted*, simply because these turn out to be meaningful levers to drive adoption or engagement. If this is your first time constructing the tree, start at the top layers to create a general model before you go deep.

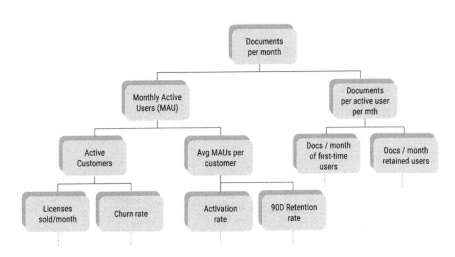

FIGURE 2.4: A Metrics Tree for the North Star Metric

The metrics tree (which is often actually a graph) shows the connections between the most important metrics at the top and the most actionable metrics at the bottom. It's best if each product team "owns" a consistent set of metrics at the bottom of the tree, while metrics higher up the tree are the responsibility of mid-level and senior management teams. Many companies set up dashboards to track the most important metrics at each level, and meet weekly to review and discuss the trends. (For more resources about metrics and which ones are applicable to your product, check out the companion page of this book: EvidenceGuided.com/BookResources.)

Some teams will define one key metric, sometimes called the *Local North Star*, which they continuously try to improve on. For example, the customer onboarding team may focus on the *% of Customers that Successfully Onboard*, while the Search team may focus on *Click-Through Rates of Top Ten Search Results*. In fact in some quarters this may be the only key result they'll need. However, the goal is never just to grow a number. The teams should also set objectives, or team missions, for example "All customers onboard fast and successfully" or "Searchers immediately find what they're after."

Some metrics will not have one clear owner, and will be shared across teams and functions. For example, *Customer Acquisition Rate* may be influenced by the work of both Marketing and Product. Customer churn is affected by Sales, Customer Support/Success, and Product. In such cases we can use *shared goals*—goals that all relevant teams have a copy of. Another option is to build virtual teams around a goal (sometimes just for a period of time) with members from different departments.

It's a good idea to create a metrics tree also for the Top Business Metric. Invariably the two trees partially overlap (see Figure 2.5).

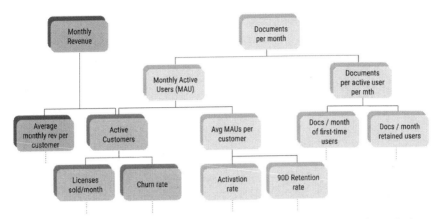

FIGURE 2.5: Simplified example of metrics trees of the North Star Metric (orange) and the Top Business Metric (green). The nodes in blue belong to both trees.

The overlap between the metrics trees shows the connection between value creation and value capture. For example, according to the tree in the example above, selling more licenses is an important way to grow the North Star Metric, and creating a sticky product that gets customers to retain is important for revenue. This sort of overlap promotes business awareness among product teams and customer focus among business teams, which greatly helps collaboration. Low overlap is usually a sign that the mission (how we deliver value) and the business model (how we capture value) are in misalignment, a problem that will be felt across the org in everything you do.

Goals Outside Your Metrics Trees

Not everything you need to do will be captured by the North Star Metric, the Top Business Metrics, and their metric trees. In fact tunnel vision on revenue and usage can lead to serious problems that are very hard to fix down the road, such as accumulation of technical debt, degrading user privacy and trust, and deterioration in company culture.

It's therefore important to add also *supplementary goals* that will keep your company and products healthy:

- Improving code health and dev infrastructure
- Ensuring the wellbeing, security, and privacy of our users

- Taking care of employee wellbeing, satisfaction, and sense of meaning
- Improving company culture, governance, and processes
- Creating a positive impact on the environment and the communities we operate in
- Ensuring the company's operations and infrastructure are serving the needs of the internal customers
- Compliance with laws and regulations
- Innovating and discovering new opportunities outside our core products

Here are examples of supplementary goals:

- O: Enjoyable, secure, bug-free user experience
  - KR: Zero security or privacy P0 issues (last quarter we had 4)
  - KR: Average customer satisfaction score of 6.0 out of 7.0 (currently 5.4)
  - KR: Launch at least twice a week (currently twice a month)
- O: Our company is sustainable, ethical, and great to work in
  - KR: Employee satisfaction score up from 4.2 to 4.5 out of 5
  - KR: 85% of our electricity comes from renewable energy (today 72%)
  - KR: Reduce average time spent in meetings from 6.5hrs/week to 4hrs/week

Rank-and-file employees are often in a good position to notice things going in the wrong direction. It's important to allow teams to create supplementary goals in their own scope of influence and to encourage employees to float missing company goals up the chain of command or directly with the leadership team.

Creating Alignment

In many companies it feels like every business unit, department, and team are pulling in a different direction and yet everyone is dependent on everyone else to do their work. Having most of the goals derived from a single metrics tree that connects everything to the top-most goal of the company is a good first step forward. It's easier to collaborate when you have a shared definition of success. However, unless you're working in a very small company, you'll need to do more to stay aligned.

Thankfully Objectives and Key Results were designed for this exact purpose. I'll show you a process to create strategic alignment across the company (although this is by no means the only way to do it). The process has these three steps, practiced at the end of each goal cycle:

1. Top-down goals (yearly)

2. Bottom-up goals (quarterly)

3. Finalizing (quarterly)

I. Top-Down Goals

Once a year the leadership team of the company or business unit kicks off the process by publishing *draft* OKRs. Depending on the size of the organization there may be 3–6 objectives, each with 2–5 key results. Fewer is definitely better—most organizations can reliably steer themselves with a 3x4 OKR limit. The OKRs clearly explain where the company should be by the end of the year. The choice of goals is influenced by the company's strategy, its values, and the most important opportunities and threats ahead.

Let's go back to the example of the company developing a smart document solution for businesses. The leaders have already set targets for the North Star Metric and the Top Business Metric, but now they have to get more specific and explain how the company will achieve this growth. Let's say that the company is seeing a multi-quarter decline in paying customers (customer churn) in the education sector, which is a key part of the company's business. The leaders decide to reverse this trend and create the following OKR:

- O: Maintain and grow our position in the educational (EDU) market
    - KR: Grow number of documents created per month in the EDU sector from 10,000 to 20,000
    - KR: Reduce EDU customer churn from 5%/month to 2.5%/month

> *Context: Over the past three quarters we have been steadily losing large education customers (>1000 seats)—both universities and schools. Our research indicates a number of potential reasons, including cheaper alternatives and dissatisfaction with the quality of the product and with our service. It is vital for the success of the company that we maintain our position as the preferred solution in the education sector.*

This concise goal shares two clear outcomes: the leaders want to grow the North Star Metric—documents created per month—in the education sector, and are asking to halve large customer churn. Note that they're not asking for revenue growth in the education sector this year; that would be a welcome side effect, but the real goal is to stop losing customers. A large part of the OKR is devoted to explaining the context: why is this goal important, and what people working on the goal should know.

This OKR comes complete with key results and targets because the leaders have all the information they need to set those. When this is not the case, the managers can start by publishing an OKR where some of the targets, or even some key results, are marked as *To Be Determined*. With this type of OKR the managers are still communicating the intent—what's the objective and why it is important—but they're soliciting the help of the company in determining the most meaningful outcomes. The answers will come during the bottom-up phase we will see shortly. Even when the OKR is fully complete, the leaders should solicit feedback from the company on whether they chose the right KRs and whether the targets are ambitious yet realistic.

Not all managers are proficient at producing such outcomes goals. If your manager is giving you OKRs that contain projects to work on (output goals), you should interview them and get to the real goal. What are we trying to achieve? What metrics would improve if we're successful? Why is this a top-priority goal? Be careful not to seem as if you're challenging their authority; you're merely trying to get to the bottom of the goal so you can do a better job. Once you've arrived at the true outcomes your managers are after, ask permission to add those to the OKR. That will put you in a good position to later come with evidence that there may be better ways to achieve the goal.

2. Bottom-Up Goals

During the year the leaders will meet at the end of each quarter to review the company goals. While changes are not common, we want to stay agile, and avoid chasing stale goals. If some of the company goals feel irrelevant or outdated, it's ok to update and republish them.

So at the end of each quarter the leaders share the most up-to-date company OKRs and ask their reports to propose OKRs of their own. It's tempting to try to create goals at each level of management and for each department and office location, but that will just overwhelm the company with planning overhead and create many redundant goals. In reality not every mid-level manager needs to create goals, and often having department-specific, or office-specific goals can hurt collaboration. A general rule of thumb is that a company of 500 employees or less can do with just two levels of goals—company level and team level, where a team is composed of up to 12 people working on a specific area. In larger orgs you should add one or more middle goal tiers. These are just general practices and your mileage may vary.

In a product team the goals will be set by the team leads—typically a product manager, engineering lead, and designer. It's important to avoid the pattern where a mid-level manager sets the goals for reporting teams. The goals that teams create for themselves tend to be much better than ones invented by managers, and they enjoy more buy-in from team members.

Here are some sample team-level goals created in response to the Educational Sector company goal:

The product team responsible for customer onboarding proposes the following OKR:

- O: All education users onboard quickly and successfully
  - KR: Reduce average EDU onboarding time from 45 days to 10 days
  - KR: Reduce the % of EDU customers that file a ticket during onboarding from 26% to 5%

The customer support team creates this OKR:

- O: EDU customers get the assistance they need to be successful and happy
  - KR: Reduce average EDU ticket resolution time from 5 days to 2 days
  - KR: Reduce the % of EDU customers that file a ticket during onboarding from 26% to 5%

The EDU Sales team offers this OKR:

- O: Maintain and grow our position as the most popular productivity suite in the education sector
  - KR: Sign at least 3 large EDU customers
  - KR: Save 3 about-to-churn EDU customers

Note how every team has adapted the OKR to its area of responsibility. Some have copied the objective as is, while others have changed it. Teams that are not directly contributing to the educational market don't have to create such OKRs, but they should take note of the goal in case they're asked to help.

Picking the right key results is part art and part science. If the team already knows which submetrics affect churn, and they see room for improvement, then those can form the key results. If the team is unsure what it can do, it may start with a goal like this one, created by the Search team.

- O: Reduce EDU customer churn through Search
  - KR: TBD

    // We're planning to conduct research (interviews, diary studies, data analysis) to determine how search may affect churn, and which metrics we should improve

There should be an agreed-upon time (usually a matter of weeks) to update this goal and add key results. Sometimes the team will discover no clear opportunities for improvement, in which case it may be better to remove this particular goal from the team's OKRs. Another option is for the team to just aim at reducing churn in any way it can, setting some guessed target. This approach is much more hit-and-miss, but still valid when the company really wants to try everything it can to achieve a certain outcome.

Setting target values for key results is yet another case of informed guesswork. If the team already has a measurement baseline and knows how the metric is trending, it can usually predict an ambitious-yet-achievable target without much problem (the accuracy of predictions is never 100% though). If it doesn't know, it can set temporary targets, with the agreement that these initial guesses may be updated up or down as the team starts testing ideas. In either case we're not going to punish the team for missing its targets or reward it for exceeding them; that will just demotivate setting honest goals. We expect the team to commit to its key results and to continuously track progress (typically every week or two), but we also acknowledge that there are things outside our control.

One way to greatly improve the odds of success is to set fewer key results. Some teams create loaded OKRs which they treat as best-effort. It's much better to trim down the goals to the strict must-haves and then commit. A rule of thumb is that a product team should have no more than four key results across one or two objectives. Fewer is better.

3. Finalizing the Goals

Team leads now share their draft goals and review them with their direct managers, and perhaps with relevant stakeholders and more senior leaders. Some discussion and negotiation will likely take place, and the goals may be adjusted. This is where middle managers play an important role. The managers should review the goals, give honest feedback, and help the team steer itself in the right direction. They may suggest that the team be more ambitious, being aware that this entails taking on more risky ideas. It's definitely ok to challenge the team's draft goals and to push back, but ultimately the goals should be decided on by mutual agreement, and definitely not dictated by the manager or the stakeholders.

The managers are in a good position to find similarities or conflicts between different teams' goals and to broker *shared goals* across teams. For example, note that the onboarding team and customer support team share a key result to reduce the number of support tickets opened during onboarding. This means they've agreed to collaborate on achieving this outcome. While I worked at Google we used this shared goals technique a lot to drive collaboration across teams, products, and business units.

The final review is with the company leadership. Sometimes at this stage the leaders get the missing key results they solicited. They may also discover important objectives that they wish to copy to the company-level goals (usually these are the supplementary goals we discussed earlier to do with the health of the company and its products). The process is therefore both top-down and bottom-up. Per Andy Grove, Intel's first CEO and the inventor of OKRs, at least 60% of key results should be invented bottom-up.

Once the goals are finalized the company can move on to execution. Note how through this process the executives are able to steer the organization without having to create plans, debate ideas, or dictate top-down solutions. The company should now be in strong strategic alignment, and yet each of its parts retains tactical independence.

Outcomes-Based Leadership

Replacing yearly/quarterly planning and command-and-control management with outcome-based goals isn't an easy transition, but organizations that make it are able to achieve much more. There's clarity of mission, strategy, and goals, and measurement of progress. Each part of the organization is working toward a concise set of measurable outcomes, for which it has full understanding and context. Collaboration is easier and more rewarding, and friction and politics are far less common. Perhaps most importantly, people are now free to discover the best ways to achieve their goals—the role of the next layers of the GIST model.

Takeaways

- The common practice of setting goals for work (output) rather than achievements (outcomes) creates high planning overhead, firm plans with little agility, and no clear definition of success. Centering goals on outcomes is both easier to do, and it allows for plan adjustments given new evidence.

- The popular process of Objectives and Key Results expresses the goal in three parts: Objective—the destination we wish to reach, Key Results—measurable achievements in this goal cycle, and Context—the rationale and supporting evidence for the goal.

- Evidence-guided companies derive their goals from models. One universal model is the value exchange loop that states that to succeed the organization needs to both deliver value and capture value; these can be measured by the North Star Metric and the Top Business Metric, respectively.

- The Top Business Metric is the metric that best represents the company's current business ambition, for example growing the amount of revenue, profit, or market share.

- The North Star Metric measures the total amount of value delivered to the market. It's an approximation, based on counting how much of the core value that the customers seek (for example messages sent, or insights gained) the company delivers per period. It's best to measure as close as possible to the value experience, and yet keep the metric simple and understandable.

- The two top-level metrics together with the company's mission statement form the company's top-level goal and can be represented as an OKR. Like with all OKRs we can set targets to both metrics and measure progress throughout the year. It's important to have two and not just one to ensure that both sides of the value exchange loop are tended to.

- The top-level metrics can be broken down into layers of submetrics creating two overlapping metrics trees or metrics graphs. This is yet another model that helps us detect the most important metrics and most actionable ones, measure where we're underperforming, and assign ownership.

- The top-level metrics and their metrics trees don't capture everything we do. There are supplementary goals also outside the trees, for example taking care of customer and employee wellbeing, the health of the products and of the company, and more.

- Alignment is crucial for success, especially in companies with lots of internal dependencies. Top-down and bottom-up alignment can be achieved through a three-step process: 1) top-down company-level OKR drafts at the end of the year, 2) Bottom-up team-level OKRs at the end of the year and of every quarter, 3) Finalizing the OKRs through a process of review and feedback that involves mid-level managers.

- This process often surfaces dependencies, overlaps, and conflicts between team goals, or areas where multiple teams will have to collaborate on a goal. These can be addressed through shared OKRs, or by forming a temporary cross-team or cross-disciplinary team to handle a specific goal.

- Switching to outcome-based goals brings many benefits, but is anything but intuitive or easy. A key success factor is establishing a clear and transparent process by which the goals will be pursued—the job of the next layers of GIST.

Notes

[1] I included references to these models in the companion page of the book: EvidenceGuided.com/BookResources

[2] "Scale-up Lessons: HubSpot's Journey from MQL to PQL | OpenView." May 21, 2018, https://openviewpartners.com/blog/hubspots-journey-from-mql-to-pql/. Accessed Mar. 1, 2021.

[3] "North Star in Action: Amplitude's North Star Metric and Inputs" https://amplitude.com/north-star/amplitudes-north-star-metric-and-inputs. Accessed Aug. 2, 2021.

CHAPTER 3

Ideas

In 2001 I assumed my first product management role. It didn't take long to realize that the most interesting part of the job is also the trickiest—choosing which ideas to build. New features and products, engineering and design enhancements, novel ways to win customers and revenue, strategic initiatives... Ideas come up all the time and from every direction. Colleagues, managers, stakeholders, customers, investors, even your mother, can (and often will) tell you what you should do with the product, and they all expect you to take them seriously because they think they have a good idea.

Unfortunately, mostly they don't.

Most Ideas Are Not Good

In the book *Trustworthy Online Controlled Experiments*, Ronny Kohavi, a long-time leader of experimentation at Amazon, Microsoft, and Airbnb, and his co-writers Diane Tang and Ya Xu, had this to say about product ideas:

> *Features are built because teams believe they are useful, yet in many domains most ideas fail to improve key metrics. Only one third of the ideas tested at Microsoft improved the metric(s) they were designed to improve [...]. Success is even harder to find in well-optimized domains like Bing and Google, whereby some measures' success rate is about 10–20%.*[1]

This result has been confirmed time and again. Slack learned that only 30% of monetization experiments show positive results.[2] At Netflix, about 35% of experiments create a measurable improvement, 19% have negative results, and 46% have no impact at all.[3] But one in three is actually a high success rate. A/B testing platforms VWO and Convert.com report that 14% (one in seven) of conversion rate optimizations run by their customers show measurable improvements.[4][5] At Booking.com experiment success rate is just 10%[6] and for Airbnb Search this number is 8%.[7]

These results are based on controlled experiments, which are our most rigorous way to test ideas. Some of the failures are caused by issues in the tests themselves, and some ideas are tested more than once. Still, these are relatively minor factors. The prime reason for failure is that the ideas tested don't create the expected effects. Many of the statistics above are taken from business-to-consumer products, but you should not assume that because you sell to businesses your ratio of success is any better. With the benefit of hindsight you can see that most ideas considered over the years (including ones requested by customers) would not have amounted to much. Across industries and business models the conclusion is the same—most ideas are simply not worth doing.

But the bad news doesn't end there.

We're Bad at Picking the Best Ideas

For us humans, it's practically impossible to predict if a product or business idea will have the desired effect months or years in advance; there are just too many unknowns. Instead, we rely heavily on our experience, intuition, backed by available evidence ("the leading competitor has this feature"). Our minds are highly susceptible to cognitive biases such as *anchoring effect* (focusing too much on one piece of available information), *sunk cost fallacy* (favoring ideas we already invested in), *false consensus effect* (assuming that the customers are like us), and hundreds more.[8] Our choices feel rational and well substantiated to us, but they rarely are.

Classic management approaches dictate picking a handful of the "best" ideas, while postponing or killing everything else. This puts ideas (and their originators) in strong contention and makes idea prioritization a high-stakes, and often political, game. Intuit co-founder Scott Cook observed the effect on company culture: "Out of a hundred good ideas, you've got to sell your idea. So you build up a society of politicians and salespeople."[9]

The decision is often left to the people in power—senior managers and stakeholder committees, but experience, expertise, and rank don't improve the odds of success. If anything, seniority may make us overly confident in our ability to conceive or spot good ideas. Many organizations lack sufficient checks and balances to critique managerial decisions and to provide feedback on their quality.

The Scientific Method

"If you want to have good ideas you must have many ideas. Most of them will be wrong, and what you have to learn is which ones to throw away." — Linus Pauling

Pauling, a renowned chemist and double Noble Prize winner, tells us how scientists come up with their best ideas. When most ideas are bad and when no one can tell which are the good ones, withholding judgment and putting multiple ideas to the test significantly raises the odds of success.

There are two specific changes you can make to bring this scientific approach into your work. The first is to generate more and better ideas through *research*. There are many techniques: interview users and observe them in their natural surroundings, analyze product and business data, evaluate competitor offerings (especially which needs they are trying to address), track market and technology trends, use your own products on a daily basis, and more.

Sometimes it's good to process what you find in group ideation sessions, hackathons, or design sprints. Some teams map out user needs and set an order of priority between them. GIST doesn't prescribe any specific research method or ideation technique, but my advice is to research continuously and to use multiple forms. As was the case with the Tabbed Inbox story we saw in Chapter 1, your research will help you uncover opportunities, set better goals, invent better ideas, and gain funding and support for your projects.

The second scientific-method-inspired change we should adopt is even more profound and yet less intuitive.

Using Evidence to Pick Ideas

Sometimes your research clearly leads to a few promising ideas which you can immediately put to the test. More commonly you'll have to choose from many competing ideas, including ones that are hard to say no to. Instead of relying on opinions, consensus, and rank, we want to pick ideas in an objective and consistent way, letting the evidence guide us toward the best ones.

Here's how it works:

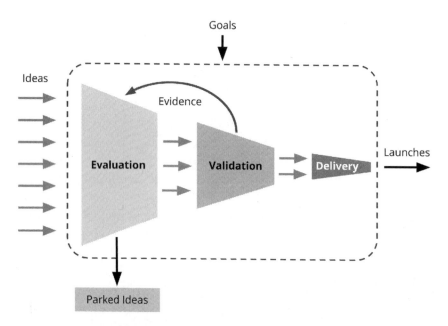

FIGURE 3.1: Using evidence to pick the best ideas

1. **Evaluate** multiple ideas quickly and objectively— In this chapter I will show you how to use *ICE scoring* (Impact, Confidence, Ease) to evaluate ideas.

2. **Pick some ideas to test**—We will use a combination of judgment and evidence to make this prioritization decision.

3. **Validate the chosen ideas**—Validation comes from testing the assumptions embedded in an idea. This is going to be the topic of the next chapter, Steps.

4. **Re-evaluate your ideas in light of the evidence you found**. Weak ideas should be parked. Ideas that still look promising should be further developed and tested again.

5. **Build and launch**—When you gain sufficient confidence in an idea (I'll explain what that means in the next chapter), switch from *product discovery* to *product delivery*. Build the idea in full, and launch.

Repeating this cycle will feed a steady flow of ideas through an engine of discovery and delivery—the beating heart of the GIST system—and will create a stream of positive-impact launches.

Keeping Your Ideas in Order

Between your research and the suggestions you get from customers and colleagues (not to mention your mother) you'll often have more ideas than you can implement. It's a good idea to keep ideas in an *idea bank*, which is simply a repository of ideas built using a spreadsheet, a database, or other data application, that can hold as many ideas as needed, indefinitely. Idea banks are not backlogs, meaning we don't expect to implement all or even most of the ideas they hold. Their main functions are to keep track of ideas, to help us compare them quickly, and to remind us that there's always more than one option.

Each product team should manage its own idea bank, tied to its scope of responsibility. Anyone can suggest an idea, but only the idea bank owner (typically the product manager) can enter it into the bank. No one likes a gatekeeper, but in my experience treating the idea bank as a suggestion box will make it unusable very quickly. The owner should strive to accept all ideas, unless they are duplicates, clearly out of scope, or unethical. Adding an idea to the bank is a weak form of commitment; it just means we'll consider the idea and nothing more. Like all GIST artifacts, idea banks should be fully visible to anyone within the company.

Technical ideas that don't directly impact any of the team's metrics (for example, re-factor module X, or upgrade to a newer version of a software framework) should not be placed in the idea bank. These should be collected and prioritized separately by the engineering lead. We will see how to allocate resources for both types of ideas in Chapter 5. However, larger engineering and design initiatives that should have clear user/business outcomes, for example doing a full redesign, should go into the idea bank.

Idea banks, like bug databases, can grow large and unmanageable very fast. It's important to continuously process incoming ideas and to move them into the right state. After an initial evaluation, or *triage*, you may choose to *park* some ideas, which means you choose not to work on them further right now (it's good practice to explain your reasoning in the idea record). Parking is the right choice for the majority of incoming ideas. You should keep a much smaller list (typically no more than 40) of *Candidates*, which are ideas you wish to investigate further. From time to time, say once a quarter, you should go over the Candidates and Parked lists and decide whether to demote or promote some ideas from one to the other.

When you define your quarterly goals, you should pick a *Working-Set* of three to five ideas to test per key result. These ideas can come from the Candidates list, or are generated on-demand through research and ideation. These are the ideas that you'll test and eventually launch, if they show good evidence. To see this process in more detail, head over to the companion page of this book, EvidenceGuided.com/BookResources, where you'll find a fuller explanation. As always, this is just an example process, and you may come up with a different one that suits your context better.

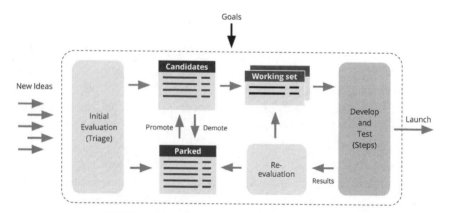

FIGURE 3.2: Idea states implemented through idea banks

To reduce your workload I suggest spending just a few minutes evaluating each new idea during the initial triage and go deeper when evaluating your candidate ideas (for example by collecting data, conducting reviews, and developing models). The product manager will usually carry the brunt of the work of evaluating ideas, sometimes aided by the team leads. You definitely don't need to bring the entire development team or any managers or stakeholders; this will just serve to slow the process down and waste the time of many busy people. These folks can review your decisions later and challenge them if they disagree.

ICE Scores: Evaluating Ideas on Their Own Merit

Evaluating ideas and choosing an order of priority are things that our brains and decision-making processes are naturally not good at. Over the years people have proposed various unbiased approaches. In this chapter and throughout the book I'll use *ICE (Impact, Confidence, Ease)* invented by Sean Ellis; however, GIST can work with other methods such as RICE (Reach, Impact, Confidence, Ease) as long as the principles I'll explain are held. Even if you're familiar with ICE, I recommend that you read the next parts of the chapter; you're likely to find things you're not currently practicing.

With ICE, each idea is assigned three numeric attributes: *Impact, Confidence*, and *Ease*, each in the range 0–10. A fourth value holds the *ICE score*, which is simply the three values multiplied together:

ICE Score = Impact * Confidence * Ease

Idea	Impact [0–10]	Confidence [0–10]	Ease [0–10]	ICE Score [I x C x E]
Community tab	7	2	8	112
New submit flow	5	5	3	75
Add PayPal billing	8	1	5	40
Double opt-in	1	4	3	12

FIGURE 3.3: An idea bank using ICE

Trying to quantify ideas with numbers sounds like a meaningless exercise to many. Ideas are amorphous and loaded with nuance; you should evaluate them through discussion, not a spreadsheet, they argue. This is a very valid point. In fact that's exactly the goal of ICE—to facilitate a *structured discussion* focused on how much the idea is going to contribute to the goals (Impact), how easy it is going to be to implement (Ease), and how sure we are that these projections will come true (Confidence). In my experience this discussion will be far more productive than the usual debate on whether an idea is good or not. Answering the questions with numbers forces us to be more deliberate and clearer, but you can also just use Low/Medium/High (don't forget *None* for Impact, as we saw that's the case with most ideas).

The one number you should be most suspicious of is the ICE score. The ICE formula is simplistic, and just sorting ideas by ICE scores can lead to naive decisions. I'll explain what I recommend doing instead later in this chapter.

To see ICE in action let's look at a real-world example. Say that your company sells antivirus/malware/ransomware security solutions to large enterprises. Your North Star Metric is the number of customer computers and devices that are fully protected against all the latest threats. Today, customer employees have to install and update your software manually on their phones. An idea was proposed to develop a centralized solution to push the software to employees' mobile devices. Customer support has flagged mobile deployment as a top customer issue for a number of quarters, and this idea has come up a few times as a Sales request. None of your competitors have this capability.

Should you build this feature?

You probably already have an intuition, but let's see how things look through the lens of Impact, Confidence, and Ease.

Impact

Impact is an estimate of how much the idea will improve the target metric.

What is the target metric? That depends on your goals. You can evaluate impact on the company's North Star Metric (for example *Message Sent* for WhatsApp or *Nights Booked* for Airbnb), which will keep the bigger mission of the company in mind and create greater alignment with other teams. You can optimize for your team's Local North Star Metric (for example *% of Successfully Onboarded Customers* for the Onboarding team), which will likely be easier to calculate, but may lead to local optimization (improving your metric, but messing someone else's). You can also pick a key result, taken from the company's yearly OKRs or from your team's quarterly OKRs (see Figure 3.4).

Teams focused on capturing value, for example an Ad Monetization team, have the same options, but taken from the *Top Business Metric* tree (for example, *Total revenue, Revenue from rich media ads*, and *Rich media ad click-through rate*). Teams who work on both delivering value and capturing value should maintain two idea banks, each ranked according to the relevant metric.

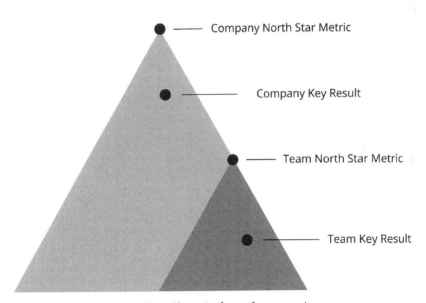

FIGURE 3.4: Alternative forms of target metric

Estimating Impact

Impact is where most of the uncertainty lives, so it is the hardest of the three parts of the ICE score to estimate. It's impossible to predict impact accurately, the number is always a guess or a projection, so don't strive for perfection.

Here are a few ways to go about it, from easiest and least accurate to hardest and most precise:

Guesstimates—At a very basic level, we may assign impact simply based on intuition, experience, and logic. Squint at the idea for a moment, then write down the number that pops into your head. If you're triaging new ideas with others, you can average the estimates (but avoid going into a long debate). Obviously, these guesses will be very inaccurate and subject to biases, but that's okay as long as we set a low value for *confidence* (more on this below).

Have a look again at our example idea: *Centrally-managed antivirus deployment for mobile.* Purely based on intuition, what impact score would you assign it with respect to the company's North Star Metric: number of computers/devices protected?

If you're like most people, you're probably thinking that this idea sounds important, so you'd give it a relatively high-impact score, say **8 out of 10**. That's a legitimate guess. However to be consistent in your guesses, you may wish to use an impact scale like the one shown below (Table 3.1):

Change in Metric	Impact [0–10]	Impact [T-shirts]
> 200%	10	X-Large (most rare)
120%–199.9%	9	
80%–119.9%	8	Large
40%–79.9%	7	
25%–39.9%	6	Medium
15%–24.9%	5	
8–14.9%	4	Small
4%–7.9%	3	
1%–3.9%	2	X-Small
0.1–0.9%	1	
0% or less	0	None (most common)

TABLE 3.1: Example impact scale

The scale obviously depends on the product and metric you choose. In some cases an improvement of 1% will be considered high impact, while in others 20% may be considered only a medium improvement. When you create your own impact table imagine 10 out of 10 as the maximum impact possible for a single idea, and organize the other levels accordingly.

Past ideas—It often helps to think of similar ideas you've tried in the past. While different, they can help you recall challenges and benefits that are relevant to this idea too.

Assessment and fact-finding—Discussing the idea with colleagues and digging up relevant data, can give you deeper insight without leaving the building.

In our example, after a bit of fact-finding, you have this new information: Employee mobile phones account for 35% of all the devices corporate customers need to protect. Different enterprises use different mobile software deployment solutions. The most common system is used by about 40% of companies. Beyond that you will have to implement a series of point solutions for each customer. Despite the hassle, 89% of customer employee phones are protected today.

Given these new facts, the idea may look a bit less glamorous. Let's say we downgrade it to an impact of **6 out of 10**.

Back-of-the-envelope calculations—A quick and rough calculation can often bring your estimates closer to reality. Here's a simple model you can build for the mobile security software deployment idea (Table 3.2):

Variable	Guess/Data
% of customers that will install the solution	50%
% mobile devices out of all devices to protect	35%
% of mobile devices not protected today	11%
Total growth in number of devices protected (the NSM)	50% x 35% x 11% = **1.9%**

TABLE 3.2: Example back-of-the-envelope calculation

So, according to this calculation, the total improvement in the North Star Metric is around 1.9%, which in our table maps to a medium-low impact of **4 out of 10**.

The calculation is based on a mix of facts and guesses, but these smaller guesses are easier to make, and likely more accurate than your first guess of overall impact. Doing this kind of exercise may be hard the first few times, but you'll soon build the skill and do it more effortlessly.

Simulations—If you wish to take your model a step further, you can try entering worst/medium/best values just to get a feel for the range of impact. You can go deeper by running *sensitivity analysis* (built into Microsoft Excel, an optional add-on in Google Sheets) and *Monte Carlo simulations* (available in data analysis tools). Best to save those for high-potential, high-cost ideas.

Test and experiment—Ultimately, the most reliable way to assess impact is to test the idea with your users. We will see how in the next chapter, Steps.

Some ideas create impact by preventing a drop in our target metric. For example, we may worry that an important customer will leave if we don't build a particular feature it requests. We can assess the impact of these ideas in exactly the same ways, and then look at the number in absolute. For example, an idea that prevents a drop of 5% in our target metric will have an impact of **6 out of 10** according to Table 3.1.

Ease

The second element of ICE is Confidence, but for the sake of clarity I'll first explain what *Ease* is. Ease is an estimation of how hard or easy it is going to be to implement this idea in full. Ease is typically the inverse of effort (person-week)—low ease means high effort and vice versa. Typically, we'll count engineering and design work as this is the scarcest and most expensive resource. When you're estimating Ease, consider how long it will take to build the whole idea *in full* (production-ready) without stopping to test it.

Similar to Impact, Ease can be guessed, derived from comparable changes made in the past, or estimated by breaking the project into its parts. We can go deeper by conducting technical investigations and building proofs of concepts (POC), and our estimates will further improve the more we validate the product.

Again, it's useful to have a mapping table like the one shown in Table 3.3, but each team should build its own scale based on its own velocity.

Person-weeks	Ease [0–10]	Ease [L/M/H]
< 1wk	10	Very High
1–2 weeks	9	
3–4 weeks	8	High
5–6 weeks	7	
6–7 weeks	6	Medium
8–9 weeks	5	
10–12 weeks	4	Low
13–16 weeks	3	
17–25 weeks	2	Very Low
26 weeks or more	1	

TABLE 3.3: Example Ease table

Going back to our antivirus/anti-malware mobile deployment idea, let's say that the team comes back with an estimate that implementing the solution that will address 40% of customers will take 12 person-weeks. That alone makes it medium-low ease, but you estimate you'll need to at least double that, or 24 weeks, to provide a solution that most of your customers can use. That puts ease at **2 out of 10** according to the table.

Confidence

Multiplying Impact by Ease should theoretically surface the ideas that give us the best bang for the buck—high impact and low effort. But life is never that easy. Psychologists Daniel Kahneman, Amos Tversky, and Dan Lovello discovered a phenomenon they called the *planning fallacy*:[10] individuals and teams tend to be overly optimistic about future projects and tasks, underestimating time, costs, and risks, and at the same time overestimating the benefits. We've all seen this bias in action. I personally fell for it many times. The planning fallacy can seriously derail our impact/ease analysis.

Confidence is the antidote to the planning fallacy (as well as many other cognitive biases). Confidence asks the question, "How sure are we that the idea will have the expected Impact and the projected Ease?" Lower confidence scores indicate lower certainty. A score of 10 indicates absolute conviction.

But how do we calculate confidence?

Again, we can take inspiration from the scientific method. Scientists don't sit in a conference room and convince each other with opinions. Confidence in an idea stems from *supporting evidence*—facts, data, and experiment results. There are many types of evidence we can collect; however, they're not all created equal. If idea A is considered good because the leading competitor launched a similar feature, while idea B was successfully tested with users, we should definitely have higher confidence in idea B. Confidence should therefore factor both what evidence we have and how *strong* it is.

To help you weigh your evidence, I created a tool—the *Confidence Meter*—shown in Figure 3.5. It lists common types of evidence you may find and the level of confidence they provide. I structured the tool to work a bit like a thermometer. It goes from near-zero confidence (deep blue) to high confidence (deep red). You can download the Confidence Meter in spreadsheet format in the companion page of this book: EvidenceGuided.com/BookResources.

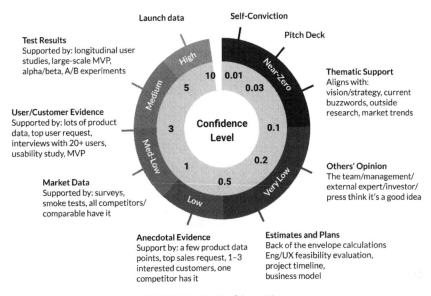

Test Results
Supported by: longitudinal user studies, large-scale MVP, alpha/beta, A/B experiments

User/Customer Evidence
Supported by: lots of product data, top user request, interviews with 20+ users, usability study, MVP

Market Data
Supported by: surveys, smoke tests, all competitors/comparable have it

Anecdotal Evidence
Support by: a few product data points, top sales request, 1–3 interested customers, one competitor has it

Thematic Support
Aligns with: vision/strategy, current buzzwords, outside research, market trends

Others' Opinion
The team/management/external expert/investor/press think it's a good idea

Estimates and Plans
Back of the envelope calculations Eng/UX feasibility evaluation, project timeline, business model

FIGURE 3.5: The Confidence Meter

Let's look at the categories of evidence up close and how they apply to our example idea—centrally-managed antivirus deployment for mobile.

Self-Conviction

Feeling strongly that your idea is good should give you little or no confidence no matter how smart you are, what track record you have, and what position you hold in the company. We all fall in love with our ideas, that's just who we are. Behind every bad idea there was someone who thought it was great.

Example Idea—On initial evaluation we estimated that this idea will have an impact of 8 and ease of 2. This was entirely a matter of opinion and logic so we only get the confidence boost of *self-conviction*: **0.01 out of 10**.

Pitch Deck

Creating a slide deck or other document that explains the idea in clear terms is not a bad thing. It forces you to think deeper and broader, and sometimes that alone helps improve or eliminate an idea. However, you're still in one-person-opinion land, hence near-zero confidence.

Example idea—No pitch deck created, so no added confidence here.

Thematic Support

Showing that the idea is aligned with some higher theme—the company's vision/mission/strategy, a current trend or buzzword in the industry, or external research—can make us feel that we found a winner ("This idea is about artificial intelligence and VR! What are we waiting for!"). However, such themes are general, abstract, and ever-changing. Worse, they're very bad at predicting the future, which is why thematic support yields very little extra confidence.

Example Idea—Let's assume mobile phone security is currently a hot topic in the industry, which supports the notion that push-distribution to mobile is of high impact. Our confidence level grows by **0.05**.

Others' Opinion

Getting colleagues, managers, or experts to support your idea feels great. Reviewing and debating the idea will likely broaden your perspective and help you uncover flaws. Unfortunately, no one has a crystal ball and your colleagues and managers are not true representatives of your users. Groupthink and politics may add new biases and lead to wrong conclusions. The 60–90 percent of ideas that research shows are bad all survived the test of peer review. So, we must look for much harder evidence before we can feel confident.

Example Idea—Let's say that managers, the team, and stakeholders are in agreement with our assessment of 8 impact and 2 ease. The idea gets a confidence boost of **0.1**.

Estimates and Plans

At this point, you've started evaluating the idea through back-of-the-envelope calculations, simulations, detailed cost estimates, or business modeling. Often these involve looking up facts and data. If the idea still looks good, you should gain more confidence. However, it's mostly guesswork mixed with sparse data, so not strong proof yet.

Example Idea—Based on team evaluation we came to estimate that Ease is going to be low: 2 out of 10. For impact, we constructed a small back-of-the-envelope model, based on facts and guesses, that suggested a value of 4 out of 10; half our initial estimate of 8 (refuting evidence). We could have chosen to reject the evidence and stick with our original estimate, in which case we'd get no confidence boost. But we chose to update the impact estimate based on the model, and thus got a confidence boost of **0.3**.

Anecdotal Evidence

This is the first category of evidence that comes from external, rather than internal, sources: a few corroborating product data points, a handful of customers who voiced interest, sporadic sales requests, a competitor that has implemented this exact idea. Anecdotal evidence is important; it shows that at least some people out there (or some data) agree with the idea. However, we humans can easily see patterns in the noise. A few data points, even if they all independently support your idea, don't prove strongly that the idea is good. Other types of external evidence are required.

Example Idea—This specific feature came up as a sporadic sales request (it appears from time to time, but also quickly disappears). This evidence is consistent with our impression that the idea will have a medium-low impact of 4 out 10, so we give ourselves a confidence boost of **0.5**.

Do we need to find every type of evidence for every idea?

No, absolutely not. As we'll see in Chapter 4, how much you need to validate an idea before switching to delivery depends on its cost and risk. For low-risk ideas we can stop lower on the confidence scale, sometimes even at expert opinion. For cheap, yet risky ideas, you can skip directly to the end and do a high-confidence test. For expensive and risky ideas you'll want to start at the bottom, and move up until you reach medium-high confidence. But in no case should you consider the Confidence Meter a checklist where you need to go through every category of evidence.

Market Data

Surveys, smoke tests, and competitive analyses help us gauge the demand in the market. We get bigger samples of external data, and for the first time we're able to define hypotheses and construct simple tests. These are important tools that you should use; however, they are fairly limited in what they can tell you—there's a big difference between indicating interest in a product on a fake landing page and actually buying it. For this reason, we still consider the confidence level medium-low.

Example Idea—We haven't found this type of evidence yet.

User/Customer Evidence

This category of evidence takes you a step further by backing up the idea with significant amounts of product or support data, customer interviews, or early tests such as a usability study or a concierge test.[11] This is much stronger evidence than anything we've seen so far, although it can still produce false signals.

Example Idea—Mobile deployment keeps coming up as a top customer support issue, which offers evidence that customers have a need for *a* solution. However, this evidence doesn't clearly support our specific idea (central deployment). It's possible that there are other, better ideas. It's also possible we will build this idea and not solve the issue. So in this case we can use a factor, say 0.5, to show that evidence is not conclusive. We get **0.5 x 2.0 = 1.0**.

Test Results

This category of evidence is the most rigorous, short of a full launch. It covers mid-level tests (for example a longitudinal study or an alpha) and late-stage tests (for example A/B experiments or a beta). Succeeding in these very demanding tests should give us a lot of confidence in our idea.

Example idea—We haven't tested yet, so no confidence boost.

Launch Data

Just because an idea is launched we should not assume it is good. This is not the time to lower your guard. To gain full confidence during and after the launch (and barring novelty effects), the new change should get consistent usage, positive customer feedback, and the target metric that we aimed for should indeed improve.

Example idea—not launched yet, so certainly we can't claim this type of confidence.

Example Idea Confidence Summary

Our total confidence score is: 0.01 + 0.05 + 0.1 + 0.3 + 0.5 + 1.0 = **1.96 out of 10**. This number is obviously not exact, but it places this idea in the area of **medium-low** confidence.

Banishing the Battle of Opinions

Imagine assessing the mobile antivirus deployment idea the old way. A group of smart people gets into a room and debates pros and cons. For one person, this idea sounds crucially important—you hear about mobile viruses all the time, and it's also the top thing that customers are complaining about. What are we waiting for? For another, an expensive project that delivers only a partial solution sounds like a big risk. A third person may dislike the idea simply based on experience and intuition. A fourth considers the idea from a political perspective—it competes with her pet project. The debate can rage on for hours and days. The final decision may be suboptimal.

Now imagine that same discussion, but this time it starts with the product manager analyzing the idea from the perspective of ICE:

- **Impact is estimated to be medium-low** (4 out of 10), based on available data and a model.

- **Ease is estimated to be low** (2 out of 10), based on team assessment.

- **Confidence in these impact and ease assessment is medium-low** (~2 out of 10)—Our strongest evidence is customer support requests, and sporadic sales requests.

Now we can hold a discussion: what should we do with this idea? Build and launch in full with no further testing? Park the idea because we have more promising ones? Keep testing and evaluate again based on the results? There's no one right answer, we still have to use our judgment and experience.

ICE moves us from shallow, subjective thinking toward deliberate, objective analysis. Impact brings the goals into the conversation and forces us to reckon what's realistic to expect. Ease reminds us to consider costs and complexity. Confidence—as measured by the Confidence Meter—helps deflect opinions and weak evidence. You'd be amazed how much more efficient the discussion gets. I've witnessed ICE shorten a debate that would otherwise rage on for a full hour into mere minutes. Participants often come out happier and comment that they feel they made better decisions.

ICE is also an important tool for communication, up, down, and across the organization. If a manager or a stakeholder feels strongly that a certain idea is good, convincing them with opinions will likely not work. Talking concretely about the Impact, Ease, and especially Confidence of an idea can bring that discussion to a better resolution. Many business teams complain about product managers making "black-box decisions" that lack clear reasoning. With ICE, not only can the decision be transparent, but the business team can also join in the effort of collecting supporting evidence and validating the idea.

Choosing among Multiple Ideas

You now know how to calculate ICE scores for all your ideas. It's tempting to sort the list by ICE score and pick ideas from the top. While this is a consistent and largely unbiased way to choose ideas, it also presents several major problems. Most ideas, including good ones, start with low-confidence values, simply because we haven't validated them yet, so they may struggle to be picked. An even bigger issue is that the ICE scores are quite unreliable as long as confidence levels are low; they can fluctuate and change strongly given new information (we'll see an example in Chapter 4). So, for the most part, you should consider ICE scores as mere hints.

Here's an alternative way to prioritize. At any given point you'll need to pick some low-confidence ideas for early validation (typically handled by the product manager), some medium-confidence ideas for early testing (requiring other team members to help), and a few high-confidence ideas for advanced testing and delivery (requiring heavy engineering and design investment). Keeping all three funnels full ensures you never run out of ideas to work on. So you can split your list of candidate ideas into these three groups by level of confidence, and pick ideas in each.

How do you pick? You can use a mix of your own judgment and the ICE values. To stay fair and consistent, go for the ideas with the highest ICE scores in each confidence group, but if you see an idea you believe in, feel free to pick it out of order. Sometimes you'd want to pick ideas based on their level of ease, for example because you're looking for some quick wins, or their estimated impact, because you're looking for ambitious ideas to hit a stretch goal. In some organizations you may have to pick an idea just because a senior or influential person requests it. This shouldn't be a problem as long as these are rare occurrences. In any event, picking an idea does not mean committing to building and launching it, but rather putting it into validation and acting on the evidence. No idea should be exempt from this rule.

ICE Is Not Enough

When I teach the GIST model, ICE gets people most excited. It's easy to think of ICE as the magic solution that will help you find the best ideas. Unfortunately, ICE alone will not do that. The real magic comes from continuously conducting research, from evaluating many ideas, and, most important, from putting promising ideas to the test and acting on the evidence. It's this last part that I see companies struggle with the most; a challenge we will tackle in the next layer of GIST, *Steps*.

Takeaways

- Most ideas fail to create a measurable improvement, but all cost us in multiple ways.
- Our brains and decision processes are bad at picking the good ideas from the bad.
- Continuous research ensures that our ideas are grounded in the needs of our users, the realities of the market, and the capabilities of the technology.
- To find the best ideas we have to continuously evaluate and validate many ideas. We park the ideas that fail in tests and invest more in those that show supporting evidence.

- Impact Confidence and Ease (ICE) helps us evaluate ideas on the basis of their contribution to the goals, their costs, and the level of supporting evidence.

- Impact and ease can be estimated in various ways—from course guesswork, through modeling, to tests.

- Confidence in an idea shows how sure we are it will create the projected Impact with the estimated Ease.

- To estimate Confidence we look at supporting evidence and the strength of that evidence. The Confidence Meter helps you do both.

- Using the language of ICE can shorten debates and make rational decisions that are grounded in reality. ICE also helps in internal communication.

- While ICE helps us evaluate ideas, its effects will be limited without the other two components of the system: continuous research and iterative idea validation.

Notes

[1] Kohavi, Ron, Diane Tang, and Ya Xu. 2020. *Trustworthy Online Controlled Experiments: A Practical Guide to A/B Testing*. Cambridge University Press. https://experimentguide.com/ Chapter 1.

[2] Fareed Mosavat on Twitter: "7/ Even with all this experience…" Jan. 29, 2019, https://twitter.com/far33d/status/1090400421842018304

[3] "Consumer Science & AB Testing | Jen Dante" https://youtu.be/pDjDMuwQuWo?t=207, Women Who Build Conference, Nov. 2017.

[4] "CRO Industry Insights from VWO's In-App Survey Results." March 9, 2020, https://vwo.com/blog/cro-industry-insights/. Accessed Apr. 9, 2020.

[5] "Why Your A/B Tests Are Failing - CXL." Aug. 28, 2014, https://cxl.com/blog/ab-tests-fail/. Accessed Apr. 9, 2020.

[6] "Stefan Thomke: Building a Culture of Experimentation" – Harvard Business Review https://hbr.org/2020/03/building-a-culture-of-experimentation

[7] "A/B Testing Intuition Busters," Kohavi et al, https://bit.ly/ABTestingIntuitionBusters

[8] "List of cognitive biases – Wikipedia." https://en.wikipedia.org/wiki/List_of_cognitive_biases. Accessed Apr. 10, 2020.

[9] Ries, Eric. 2011. *The Lean Startup: How Today's Entrepreneurs Use Continuous Innovation to Create Radically Successful Businesses*, Currency, p. 33.

[10] "Planning fallacy – Wikipedia." https://en.wikipedia.org/wiki/Planning_fallacy. Accessed Apr. 14, 2020.

[11] We'll talk about concierge tests as well as many other types of idea validation in the next chapter, Steps.

CHAPTER 4
Steps

In 1998 a software engineer named Greg Linden was struck by an idea. Linden was working for an early eCommerce company when he noticed how brick-and-mortar stores were encouraging impulse buying by displaying small items—bars of chocolates, packs of candy—in the checkout lanes leading to the cash registers. "Can we do the same in an online store?" he wondered. He imagined displaying extra items, personalized to buyers' taste and shopping history and addable with one click, in a sidebar next to the shopping cart. Intrigued by the idea, Linden hacked together a prototype and demoed it to colleagues. The reaction was generally positive, but one senior VP of marketing objected strongly. It was all well and good to show extra items to customers in physical stores, he argued, but in an eCommerce site there's a risk of distracting shoppers and causing them to abandon the purchase. Flexing his corporate muscles, the SVP prohibited Linden from launching the feature.

Normally that would be the end of the story, but not this time. This particular company was Amazon, and by 1998 it already had the ability to experiment online. Linden didn't launch the feature, but he did run an A/B test in secret. The results came back clearly in favor of the new idea: checkout recommendations generated significant extra spend per customer, and Amazon was losing money by not having the feature. Given this evidence the senior VP backed down and the feature was rushed out. Shopping cart recommendations have remained part of the Amazon store ever since and are now a staple of eCommerce.[1]

Learning and Evidence-Guided Decisions

Relying on opinions and intuition, even if they come from experts, leaves us exposed to false positives (bad ideas that get the green light) and false negatives (good ideas that are rejected). The antidote is *learning.* By testing our ideas and analyzing the results, we're able to learn whether what we assume to be true is indeed true, and to make evidence-guided decisions, as did Amazon in this story.

The classic approach of launch-and-iterate pushes the testing to the end. We pay the full cost of building the new idea before any customer or user gets to see it. Per the statistics I've shown you in Chapter 3, most ideas produce disappointing results. However, once we've committed, invested, and launched, our ability to abandon the idea or make major corrections is very limited. Mostly we're motivated to call it a success and move on to the next project.

To give ourselves the best chance of success we must test early and often. This is a core principle of Design Thinking, Product Discovery, Growth Marketing, and of course, Lean Startup, where we got the model of *build-measure-learn loops.*

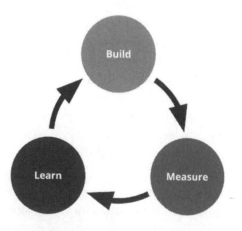

FIGURE 4.1: The Build-Measure-Learn loop

Sadly, more than two decades after the shopping cart recommendation story took place, many companies are still building too much and testing too little. Some lack know-how or infrastructure. Others feel there's no way to test their ideas short of a near-full implementation (ironically often called a *minimal*-viable-product). I also see a common fear that testing will slow down progress and get the developers stuck in research and analysis. In this chapter I'll show you how to tackle such challenges using *Steps*.

Steps: The Discovery Engine of GIST

In GIST, *Steps* are activities or mini-projects designed to develop an idea somewhat (sometimes just in concept) *and* test it. Steps can be as simple as generating projections in a spreadsheet, or as complex as running a full beta.

We saw steps in action in Chapter 1 in the Tabbed Inbox story. I came to the Gmail team with a vague idea that justifiably no one had much confidence in. We then proceeded with a series of steps: data analysis, user interviews, usability tests, dogfood... Each step gave us supporting evidence, directions for improvement, and a somewhat more complete version of the feature. From step to step we gained more confidence in the idea and were willing to invest more.

The progression wasn't fully linear. Some things we learned sent us back a few steps, and we had to throw away some code and designs. But that's exactly how it should be. It's better to discover your mistakes early when it's still easy and cheap to fix them. Eventually we arrived at a feature that was significantly better than the one we started with.

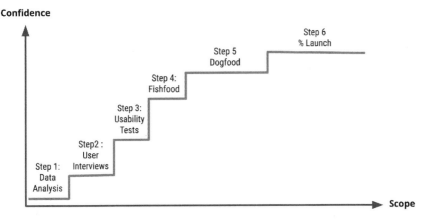

FIGURE 4.2: Example Step Progression

Per the directives of the build-measure-learn principle, we wish to make steps as short and minimal as possible. Early steps require only analysis and data collection and can be completed in a matter of minutes or hours. Some mid-stage steps (for example running a survey) require no coding and can be completed in days, but even those that do, should take no longer than a few weeks to develop, run, and collect results. As we gain confidence in the idea we'll be willing to invest more, so late steps are typically longer. The very last step is the Launch, or Delivery, step that completes the feature or product (including cleaning up any shortcuts introduced during testing) and brings it to a full launch. I'll show you a full list of step types later in the chapter.

Teams that use steps effectively start learning at a rapid pace. It's important to communicate what we've learned in a clear and simple way. ICE scores can be very useful here. At the end of each successful step we can re-estimate the Impact and Ease of the idea with *higher* Confidence and adjust our investment in it accordingly. It's also important to record what we've learned. People may leave, taking the knowledge with them, and old ideas tend to resurface. The best place to record all the learnings is the idea bank. Each idea record should link to past steps, results, and insights. In this sense, the idea bank is not just our repository of ideas, but also our knowledge base of learning.

Let's look at an example to see how all of this works in practice.

The Chatbot and the Dashboard

Let's say you manage a product that helps small businesses support their customers—informing them of the latest offerings, answering their questions, and providing any type of assistance. Your North Star Metric is the number of interactions carried out between your customers and their end users via the service, each month. However, the NSM isn't growing quite as fast as you'd like and many customers are churning or using the tool infrequently. A series of customer interviews shows that many don't find enough value in the product compared to email and instant messaging. But the interviews also surface challenges in these basic solutions. The business owners spend a lot of time messaging back and forth, and they often miss important messages in their loaded inboxes and messaging apps.

Based on this research you come up with two big ideas:

- A *dashboard* to show the business owner a summary of open and resolved requests, top issues, and messaging statistics. The dashboard is meant to help the user stay on top of things, and focus on the most important issues.

- A *chatbot* to help the business owner automate communication with their customers, intelligently answering common questions like what the opening hours are, or what's on today's menu.

A handful of customers have asked in the past for a dashboard-like feature and you feel it has good potential, but your colleagues and managers disagree. They believe only customers with a high communication volume will find it useful. The chatbot is an idea that your entire company loves and that management is quite bullish about—it feels like a big win for customers, it's a cool project, and yeah, chatbots are all the rage now.

Which feature would you choose?

If you're like most people (including me in the past) you'd opt for the chatbot because of the consensus. But maybe, like me, you've been burned once too often by relying too much on the opinions of your managers and colleagues. So this time you take a different approach: you withhold judgment and start validating both ideas in a series of steps.

Step I—Triage

Your first task is to calculate ICE scores for the two ideas. At this early stage, you use rough guesses based solely on what you already know and what your intuition says. (Note: we've covered how to estimate Impact, Confidence, and Ease in detail in Chapter 3. You may find it useful to follow the example with the Confidence Meter open in front of you; it's available to download from EvidenceGuided.com/BookResources.)

- Impact—You guess that the dashboard will boost retention, but only for a subset of your customers. You estimate no more than 3% improvement in the North Star Metric, which, using your impact table, gives you an impact of 4 out of 10. On the other hand, you believe that the chatbot will be a gamechanger for many customers, so you estimate 10% improvement which is an impact of 8 out of 10.

- Confidence—The chatbot has the following evidence in support of your 8 out of 10 impact assessment: self-conviction (you think it's a high-impact idea), thematic support (the industry thinks chatbots are of high value), and others' opinion (your managers and coworkers think it's a high-impact idea). Entering this information into the Confidence Meter we saw in Chapter 3, you get a total confidence value of $0.01 + 0.05 + 0.1 = 0.16$ out of 10, or *near-zero confidence*. The tool clearly doesn't place much faith in opinions. The dashboard, by comparison, has this going for its 4 out of 10 impact assessment: self-conviction (you think this is the impact it will have), and anecdotal support (a handful of customers asked for it). That actually bumps its confidence value to 0.61 out of 10, which is higher than the chatbot, but still in the area of *low confidence*. Anecdotal evidence is weak—it can make us see patterns in the noise.

- Ease—You guesstimate that the dashboard will take ten person-weeks to build and the chatbot 20 person-weeks, purely on the basis of the time it took to build similar projects in the past. You will get better estimates from the team later. Looking at your ease table (described in Chapter 3), you give the dashboard an Ease value of 4 out of 10 and the chatbot gets 2 out of 10.

Here are the completed ICE scores you arrive at:

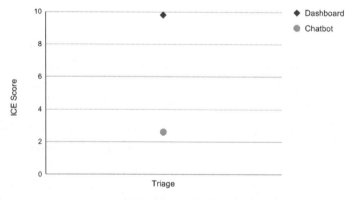

FIGURE 4.3: Step 1—Triage

The dashboard looks like the better idea at this stage. However, the Confidence Meter shows that you still haven't moved beyond very low levels of confidence. You don't have enough evidence to decide to build and launch either idea.

Why bother going through this exercise, then? Scoring ideas along the three axes of ICE makes us evaluate them in a more objective and structured way. Sometimes that is all it takes to realize an idea isn't as strong as we thought, then it's perfectly fine to park it and focus on more promising ideas. However, this is not the case here—both ideas still look solid—so, on to the next step.

Step 2—Estimates

You meet with your counterparts in Engineering and Design, and together you scope out both ideas. The engineering lead comes back with rough effort estimates: the dashboard will take 12 person-weeks to launch and the chatbot 16 person-weeks. According to your ease scale, this gives new ease scores of 4 and 3, respectively.

In parallel, you create a simple model to estimate how many customers will discover each feature, use it, and retain, and what this will mean for your North Star Metric. The result changes the numbers slightly. The dashboard looks a little less promising and so it gets a 3. The chatbot still looks like a solid 8.

Using the Confidence Meter, both ideas now pass the *estimates and plans* test and gain a confidence boost of +0.3 each. These are the updated ICE scores:

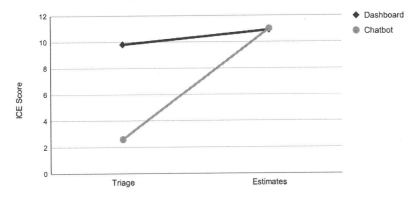

FIGURE 4.4: Step 2—Estimates

The chatbot has closed the gap with the dashboard—each now has an ICE score of roughly 11 (the decimal point doesn't really matter; these are not exact numbers.) Still, confidence levels remain low and for a good reason—these are mostly numbers pulled out of thin air. You'll need to collect more evidence before you can commit to building either feature.

Step 3—Fake Door Test

You pick two similar-sized groups of customers and give each an option to start using one of the features. Group 1 gets a new tab labeled Dashboard with a prominent yellow "New" label on it. Opening the tab shows a graphic that illustrates what the dashboard might look like, and a bit of text that calls out the main benefits. Below there's a prominent button that says, "Start using the dashboard."

Group 2 gets a change within the messaging screen in which your customers communicate with their customers. A new call-to-action appears at the bottom of the screen "Let the chatbot help you." Clicking it reveals a pop-up showing an illustrative graphic with text explaining the key benefits of the chatbot, and a button "Activate the Chatbot."

But here's the plot twist: clicking either opt-in button doesn't turn any feature on, simply because these features don't exist yet. Instead the users get this message: "Sorry, the Dashboard/Chatbot is not quite ready yet. Would you like us to inform you when it's available?". Below this message appears a button "Yes, let me know when I can use it."

This type of test is often called a Fake Door Test, or Smoke test. It measures the demand for your idea. The results pour in quickly and within a few days the data stabilizes:

- Dashboard: Only 16% of the participants chose to open the Dashboard tab, and of those that did 64% asked to be notified when the feature is available.

- Chatbot: 77% of people who entered the messaging screen clicked on the chatbot call-to-action, and of those 85% asked to be notified.

These fake door tests give us outside data to work with. The chatbot gets the full confidence boost for the Market Data evidence category (+1.0 confidence). The results seem to concur the assumption of 8 out of 10 impact. The results of the dashboard are mixed. A lower-than-expected number of people clicked into the new Dashboard tab, but then a higher-than-expected ratio asked to be notified, although these numbers were quite low in absolute terms. The team is unsure if this test measured demand in a very accurate way. You decide to keep impact at 3 out 10, but to give just half the confidence boost for the market data category: +0.5. This gives us confidence scores of 1.46 for the chatbot and 1.41 for the dashboard, and total ICE scores of 35.0 and 16.9 respectively.

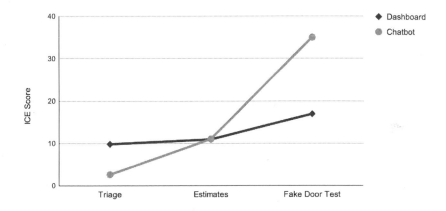

FIGURE 4.5: Step 3—Fake Door Test

The chatbot has moved into a strong lead. Your coworkers and the industry seem to have been proven right. Should you pull the trigger now? Probably not. Fake door tests are susceptible to misunderstandings and novelty effects. There's a big difference between asking to be notified of a feature and actually using it. These results surface no red flags, but they're far from conclusive proof that either idea is a winner. Keep working!

Step 4—Usability Test

To learn more, you conduct a usability test with ten existing customers, first interviewing them about their current situation, and then showing them interactive prototypes of both features. The dashboard uses canned data that is not specific to any of the participants, but is typical for a real-world user. The chatbot looks real as well, but is actually simulated by a team member seated in a different room (a Wizard of Oz test).

This round of research reveals a more nuanced picture:

- Eight out of the ten study participants, including ones with low communication volume, found the dashboard useful and claimed they would use it daily. They explain that with the noise of email and IM it's easy to miss important customer requests, or to get bogged down in supporting one noisy customer. The dashboard looks exactly like the control center they need to see the bigger picture and provide better support.

- Nine of the ten study participants said they would use the chatbot. Their level of enthusiasm was very high and many asked to have it right away. However, the test surfaced challenging usability issues in setting up the chatbot, training it, and handling handoffs back and forth with the human user. Some customers voiced concerns about offending their own customers with bot responses. Your assumptions about the sort of information the chatbot will be useful for (for example, today's menu) come into question as well, as some business owners change their offerings and operating schedules from week to week, or even from day to day.

This step gives you some food for thought. The dashboard seems to be much more valuable than you expected, and the chatbot now sounds more like a high-risk/high-reward project. Revisiting your calculation, you bump the impact scores: 6 for the dashboard and 9 for the chatbot. However, you realize that getting the chatbot user experience right will require more work. So, you reduce ease to 2. As for confidence, the dashboard gets the full boost of the User Evidence category: +2.0. The chatbot didn't pass this test quite as well and you choose to award it only half this confidence boost.

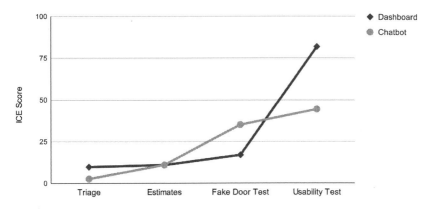

FIGURE 4.6: Step 4—Usability Test

The tables have turned yet again and now the dashboard is in the lead. You review the results with your team and your managers. Based strictly on ICE scores, the dashboard looks like the most promising idea, and now there's enough evidence to make a decision with medium confidence. The next step will likely be much more costly, so if you had to pick just one, the Dashboard would be the right choice. However, reluctant to let go of a potentially good feature, the team decides to give both ideas one more shot and continue testing.

Step 5—Longitudinal Study, and a Winner!

You build an early version of the chatbot containing just the core functionality, with very little polish. Development takes six weeks. You invite 400 of the fake door test participants who asked to be notified of the chatbot to join a two-week trial of the feature. 167 start using it; however, the number of active users drops dramatically day by day, and by the end of two weeks, you have only 24 active users. In follow-up surveys and calls, a clear picture emerges—the remaining active users are mostly happy, but other participants see the chatbot as a major disappointment. It is both harder to use and far less helpful than they had expected. Even worse, the bot antagonizes their end users, who expect a personal touch from a small business, and causes the busy business owners to work harder.

Of course, it's possible that you got this result because the chatbot was incomplete. However, analyzing the data, you and the team conclude that launching a truly useful version of the chatbot will require at least 40–50 additional person-weeks (ease of 1) and suffers from significant risks. You also conclude that the idea in its current incarnation will help far fewer customers and drive far less engagement and retention than you first imagined. You therefore reduce impact to 0.5. You have test results to back up this estimate, which gives a confidence boost of +3.0 for a total of 5.46.

Five weeks later, you launch a similar test of the dashboard to customers that showed interest during the fake door test. The results are very good. 154 participants start using the feature. Most of them keep using it almost daily with little drop-off. The feedback is overwhelmingly positive, mostly asking for more. Many participants start building daily workflows around the chatbot, and when you disable the feature at the end of the two weeks, the remaining 122 active users are gravely disappointed.[2] This is as good a result as you can expect for this sort of test. You realize that the impact is even higher than you projected—an 8. The engineering team estimates it will take another ten weeks to launch the dashboard in full, so the Ease score is now 5. According to the Confidence Meter the confidence value has jumped to 6.11 out of 10.

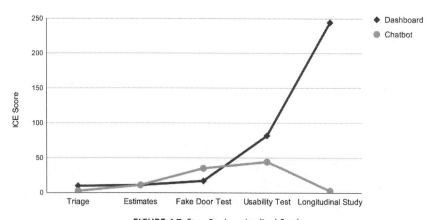

FIGURE 4.7: Step 5—Longitudinal Study

Now the decision is very easy indeed. The dashboard is clearly a feature you wish to launch and the chatbot is not. Your team, managers, and stakeholders agree. You keep the chatbot in your idea bank to record the findings, but move it to the Parked state. Perhaps in the future someone will come up with a better version of the idea and benefit from what you've learned.

Validated Learning

This story illustrates the power of evidence-guided development. The team was able to avert a costly failure (the chatbot) and focus on an under-the-radar high-value feature (the dashboard). Because of all the learning it had done, the version of the dashboard the team had launched was probably much better than the one they started with. The combination of testing, evidence, and sound judgment led the team to the right solution.

The benefits of evidence-guided development come not just from repeated testing (Build-Measure), but also from systematically analyzing the results (Learn). Recalculating the ICE scores at the end of each Step forced the team to be honest and unemotional about its ideas. Note that the three components of ICE—Impact, Confidence, and Ease—were far more helpful than the total ICE score, which created a number of false signals until Step 4. Impact and Ease helped answer the question "Does this idea still look like a good investment?", and the Confidence level answered the question "Do we know enough to choose to build and launch this idea?" You don't necessarily have to answer these questions with numbers, but you do have to be rigorous and consistent in how you approach them.

In the story the team evaluated two costly and potentially risky ideas, so they chose to run them through five steps. Smaller and less risky ideas can be processed more quickly. Minor optimizations and UI tweaks that present little risk, you can launch on the basis of expert opinion and data, or test together with other changes. Ideas that take a few weeks to develop in full can go directly into a high-confidence test like A/B experiment or Early Adopter testing. Don't be tempted to launch an untested idea just because it's easy; every idea introduces costs and risks.

With bigger, more costly ideas you want to stage your investment as the team did in the example. You start with cheap tests and invest more only if you find supporting evidence. Follow the rule: *Evidence → Confidence → Investment*. With most ideas you want to reach at least medium-high confidence levels (3.0+ on the confidence scale) before you switch into delivery mode, and with bigger or riskier ideas you should go further.

Most ideas will fail already in early steps, which means you won't have to invest much to park them. By limiting your investment in each idea you're able to give more ideas a chance, which helps defuse the political my-idea-vs-yours battles, and greatly increases the odds of finding the rare, good ideas like the Dashboard in the example. Teams that work this way consistently are likely to create a lot more value for the company and for the users compared to teams that prioritize building over testing.[3]

Choosing Steps

In this story the team chose to run the two ideas through the same five steps. I wrote it this way for dramatic effect, but of course you can run different ideas through different steps.

The key function of each step is to *validate the assumptions* (or *refute the risks*) embedded in the idea while also developing the idea somewhat. Marty Cagan lists four areas of assumptions/risks:[4]

- **Value**—Is it something that the customers need? Would it justify the cost?

- **Usability**—Can they learn how to use it? Does it fit in their lives?

- **Feasibility**—Can we build it within reasonable time and cost? Is the technology ready?

- **Viability**—Does the idea make business sense? Is it congruent with our existing business?

It's quite common to discover in hindsight that an important assumption (for example that people need another social network) isn't true. You want to surface these assumptions and to test them well before you build and launch the idea in full. Many assumptions are clear, but some are less obvious. For complex ideas I recommend using David J. Bland's Assumption Mapping[5] technique.

Once we know what we want to test, there's a wide gamut of *validation methods* at our disposal. I like to group them into five categories, from the cheapest and least accurate, to the most costly and rigorous: *Assessment, Fact-Finding, Tests, Experiments,* and *Release results* (acronym *AFTER*).

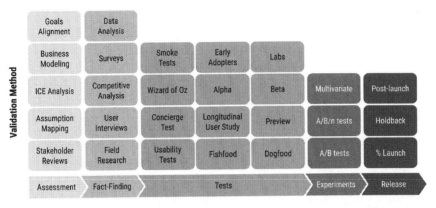

FIGURE 4.8: The AFTER Model

In the diagram above I'm showing 28 common validation methods across the five categories, but there are others, and more are being invented as we speak (you can find a detailed explanation of all these techniques in an eBook I included in the book's companion page EvidenceGuided.com/BookResources.) I didn't include technical validation techniques such as technical investigations and proofs-of-concept, but these make for good steps as well. Make no mistake—every product idea in any company can be tested (yes, that also includes your special product in your special industry). You're really only limited by your creativity and willingness to step outside your comfort zone.

Let's look at the five validation categories and how they appeared in the chatbot-vs.-dashboard story.

Assessment

Idea assessment helps us determine quickly, without having to collect external information, if we wish to proceed with an idea. Assessment is never enough to choose to go all-in on an idea (although that's the practice in many companies), but it can help us choose which ideas to test first.

In the story we saw a few assessment techniques. First the ideas were discussed with stakeholders, managers, and team members. In Step 1, Triage, the product manager calculated an initial ICE score of each idea solely based on existing knowledge and gut-feel. In Step 2, Assessment, the leads took a deeper look at the ideas. The PM created a small model to better guesstimate the impact, and in parallel the lead engineer and designer projected the Ease in more detail. Other common assessment techniques include Assumption Mapping, and Amazon's PR/FAQ reviews.[6]

Fact-Finding

Assessment often goes hand in hand with looking for supporting facts and data. These can come from data analysis, user interviews, surveys, field research, competitor analysis, and other forms of research. In the story, it's likely that during the first two steps the leads looked at usage data, for example the percent of customers that send 20 messages or more per day, and at past user research. In this case the research did show some anecdotal support for the Dashboard—a few customers had asked for it.

Fact-finding can be done on-demand, but it's best to also do it on an ongoing basis. For example, interview three to five users per week, conduct one field study every quarter, do regular data analyses, and so on. You definitely don't want to postpone all your research till the moment you need it.

Tests

Testing means putting a version of the idea in front of users or customers and measuring their reaction.

The team in the story leveraged a few types of tests. They started out with a *fake door test* that prompted people to opt-into the features in the UI. This is a typical *early-stage test*, where you "fake it before you make it." The next test, a *usability study*, also belongs to this category. The team observed user reaction to both features using interactive prototypes that relied on canned data and a hidden human operator (Wizard of Oz technique). The usability study helped the team do more fact-finding by interviewing the users. Combining techniques this way is very common.

The team then ran both ideas though a mid-stage test—a longitudinal user study. They built rough versions that were not complete, not scalable, and not polished, but good enough to be used by users for two weeks. Other types of mid-stage tests include *Alphas, Early Adopter programs*, and *Team Testing* (which in Google at least is called *Fishfood*). Again, if you're interested to learn more about any of these techniques check out the eBook included in the companion page of this book EvidenceGuided.com/BookResources.

The longitudinal user study gave the team enough evidence to make a decision: park the chatbot and launch the dashboard. In some cases, however, you may wish to proceed with late-stage tests such as *Beta Tests*, and *Preview Releases*. In the Tabbed Inbox project I told you about in Chapter 1, we relied heavily on *dogfood*—testing the feature with company employees (we had thousands of Googlers using the feature), and *Labs*—allowing users to enable the feature in whole or in parts in Settings. Late-stage tests act as dress rehearsals for the launch and also provide you with a lot more real-world data.

When you test, you have to be methodical. You have to know what data you need to collect, what to build, how to run the test, and with whom. It's important to plan tests well; we'll see how to do it in the next chapter, Tasks.

Experiments

Practically all the tests I described earlier can also be called *experiments*, but in the context of GIST I prefer to think of experiments the way statisticians do. An experiment, also known as a *Controlled Experiment*, is a special type of test that includes a control element to reduce the odds of false results. The most common type of experiment is an A/B test. We randomly assign same-size user groups A and B to use two versions of the product that are different in one variable—the label on a button, the design of a widget, the prices shown or something else. As long as we make correct use of statistical significance tests, we can say with high probability that measured differences in behavior between group A and group B, for example completing more transactions or sending more messages, is a result of the change we implemented. Other forms of controlled experiments included A/B/n tests (testing more than two versions of the same variable), and multivariate tests (testing multiple variables, say the label on a button and its position).

Controlled Experiments are a powerful technique that produces very strong evidence, which is why companies like Netflix and Booking.com run every change, no matter how small, through them. This is a good practice if you have lots of data and the necessary infrastructure. If you don't yet, start using the other techniques I mentioned and gradually build your experimentation capabilities.

Release Results

When we came to launch the Tabbed Inbox in 2013, we already had strong evidence and high confidence in the idea. Still, this was a highly visible and risky idea, and reality has a nasty habit of sneaking up on us. A product change may work perfectly in tests and then have some unexpected side effects when fully deployed (for example because you hit some edge cases you didn't encounter during testing). Instead of launching the new feature all at once, we gradually ramped up the percentage of users that got the new inbox from 0.0X% (the original testers—mostly Googlers) to 1%, 5%, 20%, 30%, and so on. This gradual rollout gave us a chance to monitor both the behavior of our users and of our system under load.

In addition to these so-called *Percent launches*, you may consider doing holdback experiments, where you launch the new change to everyone except for a small group of users, just to monitor the differences over time (you shouldn't keep the holdback folks out of the new thing for too long, though). Even after your product change is fully launched you should keep tracking the metrics to ensure the outcomes you expect materialize even when all the novelty effects have faded.

Common Challenges with Evidence-Guided Development

As powerful as combining building with learning is, it's not without its shortcomings, many of which stem from the fact that it's so different from how we're used to developing products.

"Too Slow"

You might run into the objection that combining building with learning slows down progress and causes wasted work. This is a major misconception. When you build using steps you waste less time on project plans and design marathons. The team is always focused on a "launch" that is at most a few weeks away so there's no room for procrastination, over-engineering, or scope-creep. You always build the smallest and fastest thing that will get us to learn, and sometimes this leads to the realization that you can achieve the desired outcomes at a lower cost and time. Perhaps most important, you greatly reduce the amount of work wasted on bad ideas. We saw this in action in the example where the team saved months of wasted work on the chatbot.

Learning to Learn

Adopting a build-measure-learn approach requires us to develop a scientific-like mindset that is quite different from our engineer/design/ business training, and may take time and effort to adopt.

One important skill is analyzing data in an objective and skeptical way. Steps generate data, but data is not the same as evidence. Data can be partial, corrupt, or (in controlled experiments) non-statistically significant. The test may inadvertently create a bias, or you may run into a seasonal or a one-off event like a promotion. Sometimes the results are just too good or too bad to be true. In all these cases you need to go back, fix the test, and rerun it.

Even when the results are reliable, there's a risk of biased interpretation. You should resist the urge to read the data in the most positive way (moving the goalposts), and ask honestly "what does it mean?" Most of the time you'll find that your idea created no measurable improvement, or that the results are not clear. In both cases you should assume that the idea is not working. Try to involve more people in this discussion, especially ones that have no skin in the game.

"What about the Roadmap?"

Using steps, your projects are now no longer designed to launch particular features according to a timeline; they're built to create outcomes. From time to time, we may commit to shipping a high-confidence idea on a particular date, but these should be the exception rather than the rule. This can be a challenge for companies that are attached to project plans and output roadmaps. We will talk about GIST alternatives to project plans in Chapter 5 and to roadmaps in Chapter 6. We will discuss how to drive adoption in your company in Chapter 9.

Accumulating Technical and Design Debt

Steps are designed to be minimal and quick, and typically only a very small subset of users are exposed to them. Hence we're willing to cut corners in coding and design quality in interim steps. As we progress through the steps and put the idea in front of more and more users, we want to raise the quality bar, which means paying the debt we accumulated in the earlier steps, even at the expense of slowing down the development. We should never try to rush the team into fully launching a prototype—we will pay the price later with interest.

Keeping the Team Happy

Lastly, some managers worry that their reports will not be happy with building and running tests. I can tell you from experience that projects built around steps are a lot more fun and satisfying for everyone involved. At any given point, you're working on something that's days or weeks away from being put in front of users. You can contribute an idea and see it come to life within weeks. With each successful step, the team gets a justified sense of achievement, which improves team bonding and morale. People outside the team can see the progress and take part in the success. It's a blast.

From Launch-and-Iterate to Build-Measure-Learn

Combining execution and learning isn't easy. It requires discipline to challenge your best ideas and willpower to quench your desire to build and launch them as fast as possible. Companies that develop these skills are able to innovate at a much faster rate. They're no longer invested in features and launches (output) but in user and business results (outcomes). They no longer obsess over time-to-market, but over time-to-value (the time to achieve a particular outcome). It's a profound and often uneasy transition, not least because of how output-focused we've made our development teams. In the next chapter, Tasks, we will see how to bring the developers on board and to put them at the heart of the discovery process.

Takeaways

- Building without learning exposes us to the dangers of false positives and false negatives.

- Steps bring the concept of build-measure-learn into our development processes. Each step helps us develop the idea somewhat and validate its key assumptions.

- Early steps are short and take minutes to hours, mid-stage steps may take days or weeks, late-stage steps can be even longer. Last is the Launch step which is about delivery.

- There's a wide gamut of tests from the cheapest and least conclusive to the most expensive and rigorous, as captured in the AFTER framework: Assessment, Fact-Finding, Tests, Experiments, Release results.

- At the end of each step it's important to analyze the result and re-evaluate the idea. ICE scores are helpful here. At the end of a successful step we should be able to estimate Impact and Ease with higher confidence.

- When to switch from discovery to delivery depends on the size of the idea and the risk embedded in it. With expensive and risky ideas we'd want to reach at least medium-high confidence.

- In expensive ideas it's important to avoid the temptation to invest too much too early. Start with cheap steps and only invest more when you gain supporting evidence and confidence. This way we allow more ideas to be tested, and improve the odds of finding the good ones.

- Counterintuitively, building projects around learning wastes less time and resources. There's less room for procrastination and scope-creep, we may realize we can achieve the desired outcomes with less scope/effort, and, most importantly, we spend far less on bad ideas.

Notes

[1] You can read the full story in Greg Linden's blog: http://glinden.blogspot.com/2006/04/early-amazon-shopping-cart.html

[2] It's important not to leave a version of the product that was created for limited test purposes in production. That may cause major issues for the users, and will force your developers to support this version rather than focus on discovery and delivery.

[3] For a numerical example of why combining discovery with delivery creates value faster and cheaper, see this article: https://itamargilad.com/velocity-vs-impact/

[4] The Four Big Risks—Silicon Valley Product Group—https://www.svpg.com/four-big-risks/

[5] Assumption mapping is a team brainstorming technique that helps surface and prioritize assumptions and prioritize by level of importance and by existing evidence. It is described here: https://www.precoil.com/assumptions-mapping

[6] Amazon's PR/FAQ process is described in the book *Working Backwards* by Colin Bryar and Bill Carr https://www.workingbackwards.com/

CHAPTER 5

Tasks

In early 2017, I met Nacho González and Eduardo Manchón to discuss their startup, Mailtrack. The company had developed a solution that helps email users track the levels of engagement their messages get. When we met, the service had already found product-market-fit with solo professionals and small businesses, and usage and revenue were picking up nicely. But there was a problem (there usually is one when they come talking to me): development was moving at a much slower pace than you'd expect in a 12-person startup. Nacho and Eduardo, both serial entrepreneurs with distinguished track records, were understandably frustrated. They had all these ideas and plans, but very little was launching to the market. Development was always behind schedule, and encumbered by delays and missed deadlines. The developers seemed disinterested in the success of the business, and insisted on big quality improvement projects that took up time and resources. The two founders wanted to know if I had a solution to make the engineering team work faster and be more business-minded.

Over the years I've heard similar stories and got similar requests time and again. It seems that managers are forever disappointed with the performance and mindset of their product teams. Talking to engineers and designers, I hear the other side of this story. Managers who set unrealistically short deadlines and keep changing their minds, a general disregard for code and design quality, and no real empowerment. There's a clear gap in expectations, and often, a mutual lack of trust. Even companies like Mailtrack, where managers and employees share a healthy relationship, suffer from some of these symptoms.

Could anything be done to improve the situation?

As it turns out, the answer was Yes. With some guidance, Eduardo, the CPO and later CEO, was able to make major improvements. In a matter of weeks the pace picked up, the company got into strong alignment, and generally, everyone reported being happier. What we did had nothing to do with "fixing engineering" or "improving culture," and everything to do with one of the biggest issues that plague product development today.

The Growing Divide Between Developers and the Business

When I started working as a software engineer in the mid-1990s, developing software was a much simpler thing. My manager assigned me a project, and it was my job to get it done. This meant figuring out what the software should do (requirements), how it should behave (design), and how it would be implemented (development). I conducted research, collected input from managers and colleagues, and sometimes even talked to customers. It was down to me, the software engineer, to make sense of it all and come up with a solution.

That approach to developing software looks very naive today. We now have specialized roles to divide the work: product managers set requirements, designers are in charge of user experience, researchers and data analysts take care of gathering user data, engineers are there to develop the product. Each discipline has a specific set of deliverables to create, and they often report to different managers and are measured on different things.

The mass adoption of Agile development brought major improvements in project management, but deepened yet another divide. Today, most executives, business stakeholders, and finance folk still live in what I call *Waterfall World*, which is all about business goals and multi-quarter roadmaps. Engineers and designers, on the other hand, live in *Agile World*, where the horizon is one to two weeks long and the implicit goal is to burn through story points, move tickets to the Done state, and push small increments of working code into production. Historically, Agile methods emphasized continuous delivery of *value* to customers and to the business, relying on short feedback loops with users. But, in reality, that's not the way most agile teams operate.

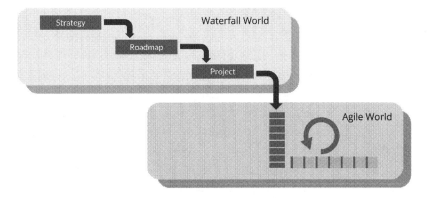

FIGURE 5.1: The two worlds

These changes gradually disconnected engineers and designers from the business, and focused them on output—delivering products and features according to a set schedule. In many companies the result is a disengaged development organization that works much like a hired contractor—asking for detailed requirements, inflating budgets and schedules, and often delivering unsatisfactory software due to lack of context. Inclusive organizations like Mailtrack that give developers a say, get big quality and infrastructure projects (some necessary and some less so) that can take months or years to complete. To be clear, this is not happening because the developers don't care, but because of the position we're putting them in. As Eduardo later pointedly put it, *we turn developers into the enemies of the business.*

Conventional wisdom has it that the solution is *product management.* Sandwiched between waterfall planning and agile execution, it's the job of PMs to make the two systems work together. On the one hand, they're expected to make sure products and features ship according to the roadmap, much like project managers. On the other, they need to feed an insatiable Agile machine with perfectly prioritized product backlogs and well-crafted user stories, keeping every engineer fully utilized. Both sides of the PM role are laborious and thankless, full of meetings, reviews, and standups, and plagued by the need to generate an endless stream of artifacts. The product managers I meet have little time to talk to users, research the market, or validate ideas. Many PMs know they're helping perpetuate a dysfunctional system, but feel helpless to make a change.

Building a Shared View of the World

In the previous chapters we saw how product teams are involved in choosing goals, finding high-impact ideas, and testing these ideas using steps. The job of the fourth layer of GIST, *Tasks*, is to translate all of those into action. Tasks are the day-to-day activities, the things we manage with Scrum and Kanban—designing a button, writing an interview script, developing a new algorithm. In GIST we're not trying to invent a new task management system; whatever agile method the team likes to use is fine. We do want to ensure that every task is connected, through the GIST stack, to the goals of the team and the company. Our aim is to have the team work with a deep understanding of the context, and to empower it to make decisions.

The first change we introduced at Mailtrack was to use a different type of product backlog—a *Step Backlog (or Step Plan* as we then called it). Here's an example:

Step	Priority	Step Doc
Mobile Labels: Dogfood	1	Link
Mobile Labels: Beta launch	1	Link
Pricing Change: A/B/C test	1	Link
Tech: Continuous delivery pipeline for Backend-PHP	1	Link
Simplified Signature: Survey	1	Link
Landing Page: 3 variations A/B/C/D test	2	Link
Continuous Delivery Pipeline for Extensions	2	Link
Monetization: Monthly plans smoke test	2	Link
Fixit Week (close top P2 bugs)	2	Link
Dashboard: Feasibility research	2	Link
Dashboard: Dogfood v0.1	2	Link
Tech: Architectural changes NextGen fpm	3	Link

FIGURE 5.2: Example Step-based product backlog

Like all backlogs, this is a prioritized list of work items from which the team can "pull work," continuously in Kanban, or per-sprint in Scrum. The key difference is that in a step backlog the work items are *idea validation steps* of the types we saw in Chapter 4, for example a data analysis, a fake door test, or a beta. You can also add technical validation steps, such as building a proof of concept, or carrying out a technical investigation. Importantly you should also include tech/design work that is aimed at achieving a technical or design goal—weeks-long projects aimed at reducing technical or design debt, laying out infrastructure, doing important maintenance work, and so on. There should be no hidden projects.

Using a step backlog is a subtle, but important change. In Mailtrack, as in other companies I've seen, the backlog was full of work items like "Complete API X," "redesign interface Y," or "build widget Z." Success meant producing working code and (at best) a demo. The goal was to "eat" the backlog to get to some big launch that is sometimes months away. Step backlogs change this mindset. Each step is a days- or weeks-long mini-project with its own "launch" to a well-defined set of users. For example: "In five weeks we'll run a usability test of features X and Y with 12 small-business owners." Working on steps enlists the team to do product discovery as well as product delivery, and connects its work to the realities of the users and the business.

At Mailtrack, step backlogs made another big difference. Up to this point the managers planned in terms of months/quarters-long features, and the team thought in terms of days-long tasks. The step backlogs created a middle-ground—a shared, and useful view of *all* the work. As Eduardo and the team created their first combined step backlog, engineering quality improvement initiatives took up most of the space. When I visited two weeks later, most were gone, or downsized considerably. When I asked Eduardo what happened he just smiled. Seeing for the first time all the opportunities ahead of Mailtrack, the engineering team realized the startup was over-investing in quality work and chose to deprioritize some of its own ideas.

This was not a one-sided change. Eduardo and Nacho—the leaders of Mailtrack and effectively its product managers—had to improve some of their own habits. Before, they tried to pursue too many ideas at the same time, and came up with new, must-have ideas from one day to the next. With step planning, the founders had to have more rigor. The backlog made it clear that the capacity of the team is limited. They could still introduce ideas at short notice—the backlog is agile—but the very first steps were usually fact-finding steps that the managers themselves owned—running surveys, analyzing data, investigating competitive products. Eduardo reported that this made him more accountable, a word, I noticed, few managers ever used to talk about themselves.

The GIST Board

Step backlogs are a good first move to get teams out of delivery mode. However, as you introduce the other layers of GIST, you may wish to use something like the *GIST Board* shown in Figure 5.3 (as did Mailtrack later on). As usual the process I'm about to show is just for reference. Your approach may differ.

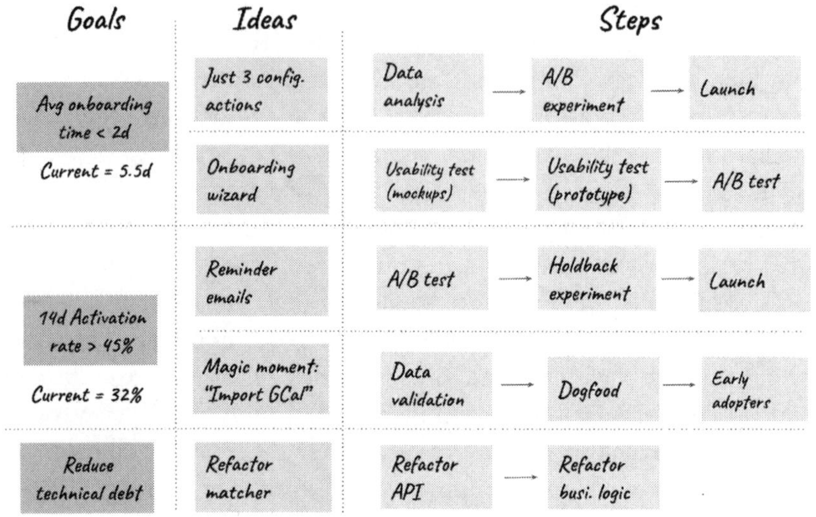

Goals	Ideas	Steps		
Avg onboarding time < 2d Current = 5.5d	Just 3 config. actions	Data analysis	A/B experiment	Launch
	Onboarding wizard	Usability test (mockups)	Usability test (prototype)	A/B test
14d Activation rate > 45% Current = 32%	Reminder emails	A/B test	Holdback experiment	Launch
	Magic moment: "Import GCal"	Data validation	Dogfood	Early adopters
Reduce technical debt	Refactor matcher	Refactor API	Refactor busi. logic	

FIGURE 5.3: The GIST Board

The board, which may be physical or digital, shows the things that the team is working on *right now*. The structure is fairly self-explanatory:

- Goals on the left—These are the outcomes the team is trying to achieve this quarter, including business, technical, and design outcomes. I recommend no more than four per quarter.

- Ideas in the middle—Put here only the ideas you're actively pursuing now; the rest can live in an idea bank.

- Steps on the right—Typically, we'll only need the next 2–4 steps per idea. We'll talk about how to create this part of the board shortly.

You may wonder where the tasks are. Usually there are too many to show here and they change on a daily basis. I suggest that you keep managing tasks in whatever tool you're using today—Jira, a Kanban board, or something else—but start referencing or linking back to the steps.

Consider locating the board physically next to the team. If you use a digital board, try to display it on a large screen; it will serve as a constant reminder of the bigger picture. I also recommend that the team meet to review the board, typically for 30 minutes, every week or two, just before the team's regular task-planning session. Yes, it's another recurring meeting, but this one will save your life. Don't make it optional; all members of the team should attend.

The agenda is:

- Go over the quarterly goals and assess progress, potentially through scoring. This is your weekly/fortnightly checkpoint that is so crucial for the success of Objectives and Key Results.

- Briefly review the ideas we're currently pursuing, and discuss if these are still the most promising ones.

- Go over the steps in order of priority and review status: are we on track? Is the step running and collecting data? Was analysis of the results conducted? Simply launching code or running a test won't make a step complete; it's still ongoing until results are collected and analyzed.

- Discuss changes to the plan—This may include updating the goals, adding and removing ideas and steps, and finding ways to help key steps complete faster. The GIST board is very dynamic and can change often, so it's best to have most of these discussions in a smaller group ahead of the meeting. Changes that were already decided on should be updated on the board before the meeting starts.

People have reported that the board and the regular meetings help them keep the bigger context in mind and prevent them from over-focusing on the tasks. The board also helps get a true sense of progress—the team can readily see if it's behind on its goals, or if it's not executing well on some steps. The board creates a useful view for managers and stakeholders too—a substitute for project plans and Gantt charts. It's a good idea to make the board fully visible to anyone in the company, and to actively share progress snapshots on a regular basis, for example in a bi-weekly email.

Managing the GIST Board

A mistake I sometimes see is putting the product manager alone in charge of the GIST board, or worse, having director-level managers manage the board on behalf of their reports. That may be empowering for the PM or for the directors, but it leaves the engineers and designers as execution workers, with all the disadvantages that come with that. The better option is to have each product team collectively create and manage its own GIST board.

A typical product team (sometimes also called a squad) will have up to ten engineers, along with their designer(s), and product manager. In some cases user researchers, data analysts, or product marketing managers may join the team (attending its regular GIST board reviews). That's a lot of people to involve in every decision, and from experience it will make for lots of unproductive meetings and very unhappy engineers. Instead, I highly recommend designating one of the engineers, a person with good knowledge of the software and the domain, the *engineering lead*. The lead doesn't manage the rest of the team, but she may guide the other developers and represent their views in planning discussions. The engineering lead, together with the product manager and designer, form the *team leads*, sometimes also called a Trio or a Triad. The leads together should manage the GIST board and make the key decisions behind it. The rest of the team should review and approve and there should be room for team members to suggest changes or push back.

Let's look at how to create each part of the board.

Choosing Goals

You want to recreate the board at the start of each goal cycle, typically at the beginning of the quarter. Start by copying the team's quarterly outcomes—the *key results*, if you're using OKR—into the left column. In Chapter 2 we saw how to use the top-down and bottom-up approach of OKRs to set the most important team-level goals. These may include hitting certain business results (for example grow 14d activation rate from 39% to 45%), but may also be about improving product quality, building better infrastructure, enhancing user experience, improving processes, and more.

There's no bulletproof way to strike a balance between product, engineering, and design goals, but the leads should come to a decision in *partnership*. Each lead will bring an important perspective, but their joint mission is to figure out what's best for the company and for the team. In some quarters this may mean putting aside quality work in favor of achieving certain high-importance outcomes (as the Mailtrack team has done). In others, the team may choose to throttle down new product development in order to get on top of important tech/design/performance/infra goals. Most quarters the mix will be somewhere in between. Having good team metrics and keeping things measurable helps clarify the priorities and avoid disciplinary agendas.

Choosing Ideas

Next, you want to pick ideas to place on the board—the ideas you wish the team to work on right now. Some ideas may be already in-flight from the previous quarter, but you should ask if these still represent the best investment. The key question is how to best achieve the quarterly goals. We saw in Chapter 3 how to rank ideas based on their Impact, Ease, and evidence-based Confidence (ICE), but this applies mostly to product ideas such as adding a workflow, or running a promotion. For technical and design ideas, the respective leads should come up with a priority, but they should be able to explain clearly (ideally with metrics) why these ideas are the most important. Sometimes it helps setting up a budget for how much you wish to invest each quarter in engineering work vs. product work.

Choosing which ideas to work on is the most contentious part of the process, and managers and stakeholders may wish to step in and push for specific ideas. As counterintuitive as this may sound, while anyone can propose ideas, it's best to leave the decision about which ideas to pursue and in which order to the team. These rules help empower the team to do that:

- The team is optimizing for achieving the goals, not for launching specific ideas.
- The team is choosing which ideas to *test* first, not which ideas to build and launch.
- As most ideas will fail in testing, there will be room to explore many more ideas.

- The team uses evidence, not opinions, to make decisions, and it does it transparently.

- The team is allowed to say "no" to ideas that fall outside the goals.

Choosing Steps

Next we want to define the set of steps through which we'll develop and test each idea on the board. In Chapter 4 we saw that the job of steps is to both move the development of the idea forward and to validate the core assumptions that underlie it.

Let's look at an example:

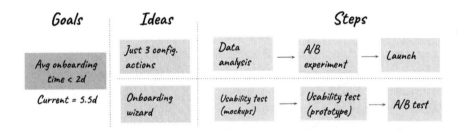

FIGURE 5.4: GIST board example

In this case one of the team's goals is to shorten the average time it takes users to onboard and start using the product to two days or less (note how the board shows that the team still has some work to do). They're pursuing two ideas in parallel. The first is to shorten the onboarding flow by reducing the number of configuration actions to just three, allowing users to become active earlier. This is a fairly simple and fast change to implement, but it's not without its assumptions or risks, which is why the team chose these steps:

- Step 1: Data Analysis—It's possible that the vast majority of users already abandon the flow during the first three configuration actions, in which case this idea will have low impact on the goal. So it makes sense to start by looking at the data.

- Step 2: A/B test—To test whether the idea is indeed shortening the average onboarding time we can run it through an A/B test, comparing the behavior of users who experience the shortened onboarding flow vs. those who get the old flow. This is also a good way to make sure that other metrics, for example 7-day retention, are not hit by the change.

- Launch—If the results of the A/B experiment are positive the team will move on to finish the implementation and launch. This includes closing any gaps or shortcuts left in the code or the design in earlier steps. Naturally we will keep tracking the metrics even after the launch to ensure there are no adverse effects in the long term.

The second idea the team is pursuing is about launching a completely new onboarding experience called the Onboarding Wizard. This is a much bigger change, and it entails important assumptions about user experience, so the first couple of steps include different types of usability tests. If those generate supporting evidence the team will proceed with an A/B test. It's likely that this idea will require more steps, including the final Launch step, but as step plans often change based on the results, there's no point trying to map out the entire project.

In Figure 5.4 I show steps arranged in a linear sequence, but that's not always how things play out. Steps can be executed in parallel and sometimes we will use one step to test multiple ideas.

Steps

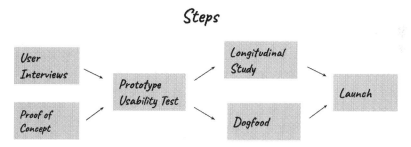

FIGURE 5.5: Steps don't have to follow a sequential order

Once the board is complete with goals, ideas, and steps, it should be reviewed by the team and updated based on its feedback.

Now we're ready for execution.

Context, Not Requirements

One morning, while we were developing Gmail's Tabbed Inbox, an engineer named Greg invited me to his desk and showed me a user interface change he created with our UX designer, Jeroen. We had just added the ability to drag messages from one tab to the next (for example from Promotions to Social) to allow users to correct misclassifications, but Greg and Jeroen felt that the experience wasn't very intuitive. Now, as Greg started dragging a message, the tabs visibly stretched and displayed a text hint, creating an inviting drop target. The effect was both very cool and very useful. I was the product manager for this project, but it didn't occur to me to ask for this change, and naturally I didn't spend any time in design discussions, reviews, and specifications. Greg and Jeroen saw a problem, iterated directly on the code, and changed the product for the better. Now they were asking for my feedback. I didn't have any, except to say that I liked it a lot. In this case, as in so many others I experienced at Google, people just did the right thing simply because they understood the context.

This last story will seem self-evident in companies like Google where engineers and designers have a major part in shaping the product, but you'd be surprised how many companies there are where developers just do what they're told and nothing more. These companies miss out on a tremendous source of product innovation and employee satisfaction, and at the same time they put a huge burden on their product managers. Don't be fooled into thinking that this is a Google-only thing; your engineers and designers are perfectly capable of working this way and you'll be pleasantly surprised by what they will come up with. While some engineers definitely just want to code, and those should work predominantly on engineering-centric projects, in my experience most developers prefer contributing to both product discovery and product delivery. It's a matter of giving them a chance and motivating them to do more than just code.

In my experience there are a few parts to the change. First we need to shift the definition of team success from pushing code to production (output) to achieving the team goals (outcomes). The constant drum beat of launching steps, and seeking user/business evidence helps drive the point home.

Second, we want team members to have plenty of context: users and their needs, business rationale, competitive situation, and more. The context helps team members understand what makes sense and what doesn't, and eliminates the need to spoon-feed them with bite-sized, detailed requirements. In fact, if there's one thing I've learned in over 20 years of product management and coaching, it's that the more detailed you make the requirements and user stories, the less likely you are to get what you expect. Jeff Patton talks about this phenomenon in his book, *User Story Mapping*: "Ironically, we put stuff in writing to communicate more clearly and to avoid risk of misunderstanding. But, way too often, the opposite is true. Shared documents aren't shared understanding."[1] He later provides this sage advice: "Go ahead and write something, anything. Then use productive conversations with words and pictures to build shared understanding."

The GIST board and the regular review meetings will help a lot in creating a shared understanding. During the discussions we will have to explain why we chose these goals and ideas, what the hypotheses and assumptions are, what evidence we have to back them up, and what we still need to validate. Even the most junior team members should come out with a good understanding of the *why*.

But just as important, we want to create a shared understanding of the *what*, using, as Patton suggests, discussions and images. We'll accomplish this by developing steps as a team.

Planning and Executing Steps

Some steps, like sending out a survey or conducting a technical investigation, require just a single person. Others require a small team, which I like to call the *Step Force*. We want to include only those people who will actively work on the step: one or more engineers, a designer, a PM, researcher or analyst, product marketing manager, and so on. Managers and coworkers may be consulted for input and feedback, but it's best that the core step force will stay small and independent.

Planning the Step

It's a good idea to kick off every step with a meeting around a whiteboard to discuss what we want to achieve and how. All the members of the step force should attend and contribute. Insights like "we can measure this in a different way," and "this is going to be hard to do" are very important.

A step is successful if at the end of it we have enough evidence to re-evaluate our idea (if you're using ICE then it means being able to estimate Impact and Ease with *higher* Confidence). That means we need to plan the step a little differently than we would a classic delivery-focused project or milestone. Typically we will summarize the decisions in a short document. Here's a high-level template:

- **What do we need to test?** Each step will test some assumptions, for example "Cluttered inboxes are a major pain for casual users," and "Shopping cart recommendations will not cause higher purchase abandonment."

- (When relevant) **Who are we testing with?** For example: "at least 300 small-business owners who are already using our product at least once a week," or "random 2% of site visitors."

- **How will we test?** This is the heart of the step doc. We can say things like: "The participants will use an interactive chatbot prototype that includes features X, Y, and Z. The prototype will be operated by a team member behind the scenes (Wizard of Oz test)." Where relevant you may add mockups, sketches, or whiteboard screenshots. You may write this part of the doc in the form of user stories or epics, if that's your cup of tea.

- **What do we need to measure?** Here we list all the data we need to collect. For example: "click-through-rate on the Buy Now button," or "share of participants who are able to complete tasks A, B, and C unassisted." Don't skip this part. Nothing is more frustrating than realizing that you have to rerun a step because you forgot to measure a key metric or to ask a crucial question.

- (Optional) **What would we consider success?** Setting targets in advance can protect us from biased interpretation and moving the goalposts. For example: "at least 10 of 12 participants are able to complete all the tested tasks with the new inbox," or "a statistically significant uplift of at least 0.5% in conversion rates."

Some teams find it useful to include one or more hypotheses statements. Here's a template taken from Jeff Gothelf's and Josh Seiden's book *Lean UX:*[2]

> We believe that [doing this], for [this target group], will achieve [this benefit].
> We'll have reason to believe we are right when we see [this measurable result].

Executing the Step

Once you reach agreement on the goals and content of the step, the members of the step force can go ahead and plan the specifics, for example recruiting participants, developing interview scripts, choosing what to develop and how, and booking rooms and other resources. It's important to stay in constant communication, and to solicit feedback, just as Greg and Jeroen did when they showed me their new design of drag-and-drop. It's definitely ok to push back when you think what's being developed is missing the mark. The point is to develop a shared understanding of what we should develop through continuous discussion, demos, and working code. In a sense, we're developing the requirements together.

As I mentioned, a step is successful if it generates results that allow us to rescore the idea with higher confidence. All the members of the step force collaboratively share the responsibility for the success of the step. To achieve this goal, step force members may have to do things that are not in their usual job descriptions. I've seen PMs conducting user research, developers helping with design and note-taking, and designers doing statistical analysis. If you've worked in a startup, this do-whatever-it-takes mode of work is probably not new to you.

Connecting Steps with Agile Development

As I mentioned, you can introduce goals, ideas, and steps while keeping the Agile development methodology that your team is using today. We've already covered how to create a *step backlog*, which is essentially the list of next steps taken from the right-most column of the GIST board, with an order of priority set by the leads. Now let's talk about how to connect with Scrum and Kanban cycles.

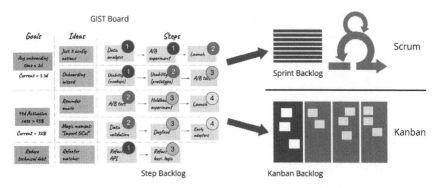

FIGURE 5.6: Connecting the GIST board with Scrum and Kanban

With both Scrum and Kanban, the team will likely want to break the product backlog into a set of smaller work items (what we call Tasks in GIST) to be placed in a *Sprint backlog* or a *Kanban backlog*. Scrum teams often use the sprint backlog to plan the capacity and content of the next Sprint. This may require all the steps included in the next one or two weeks to be defined, planned, and broken into tasks, which while possible to do, will incur lots of planning overhead. Another complication is that the step backlog can change from one day to the next: we may have to rerun a Step, or we may decide to introduce a new step based on the results we got, or we may park the entire idea with all its steps. All of this may alter the content of a sprint. One solution is to use sprints of no more than one week which reduces the odds of mid-sprint changes. A bigger meta-question for the team to discuss is how important it is to keep the content of the sprint fixed, and why.

Another common question I get is about mapping steps to user stories and epics, which many Agile Dev teams build workflows around. The good news is that it's definitely possible to express a user-facing step such as a usability test, a fake door test, or an A/B experiment as one or more user stories or epics that describe the experience of the participant during the test or experiment. However, as the developers take an active part in designing the step and in figuring out how things should work, the need for fine-grained user stories drops dramatically, which frees product managers to do other things and reduces red tape.

Getting Everyone on the Same Page

A colleague of mine at Google once described product management as herding cats—getting a bunch of people with different roles, perspectives, and life experiences to agree on what to do with the product. Reaching agreement with managers, stakeholders, and the team is undoubtedly one of the hardest parts of the job. Here's what life can look like if you have a system like GIST in place.

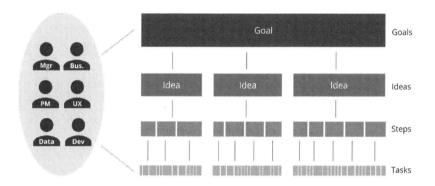

FIGURE 5.7: Collaboration through the GIST stack

Developers no longer just focus on tasks, as they realize these tasks are there to accomplish a step, which they helped define and co-own; the step is there to develop and test an idea, which they understand and maybe even proposed in the first place; and the idea attempts to achieve a goal, which they took part in setting. Much of the fog around the plan is lifted—it's no longer just a managers' game.

There's much better context in the opposite direction as well. Managers and stakeholders now understand what the product team is trying to accomplish through goals that they had a hand in shaping. They have full visibility into the list of ideas the team is considering—some of which they contributed—and how these ideas stack up. They can see on the GIST board what ideas are being pursued now. If they're interested, they can see which steps are being conducted and what results they generated. They can contribute in various ways, including helping to collect evidence and interpreting results. They get to influence the product without having to do the hard work of choosing solutions and creating plans, which frees them to focus on their main roles. As Eduardo, CEO of Mailtrack, told me "After we implemented GIST, I really started enjoying coming to work each morning."

Lastly, with GIST, product managers are no longer just roadmap and backlog administrators. They can now devote more time to studying users and the market, to leading product discovery, and to supporting delivery. Product managers that experience this new way of working never want to go back.

Basing the work on shared understanding, trust, and delegation isn't a brave, new idea. It's the old way of working that I experienced as a young engineer, but that we've since forgotten. In the book *Creative Selection*, former Apple engineer and designer Ken Kocienda describes how in 2005–2006 practically all of the revolutionary user interface of the iPhone was invented by rank-and-file engineers and designers with not a specification or user story in sight. Arguably most of the world's most successful products were built in a similar way.

Looking at the Bigger Picture

You now have a good understanding of how evidence-guided development works at team level. But what about at higher levels? How does GIST relate to company strategy, quarterly/yearly roadmaps, and big projects? We'll talk about these important questions in the next chapter, as I'll walk you through a full real-world example.

Takeaways

- Role specialization and Agile development have placed many developers in "delivery teams" that are focused on output. Those teams are severely disconnected from the needs of the business and the realities of the users.

- Putting product managers between the planning and the execution doesn't fix the problem. The PMs work very hard just to deliver the roadmaps and feed the agile team with backlogs and stories, but this isn't a truly agile system, and its main focus is output.

- A good first step to get the team out of delivery mode is to switch to a step backlog, where almost every work item is an idea validation step or a pure engineering/design enhancement step.

- Teams that use the full GIST stack would benefit from using the GIST board—a simple work management tool that shows the current goals, ideas, and steps the team is pursuing.

- The GIST board should be created and maintained by the team leads (AKA Trio or Triad), but shared broadly and reviewed regularly by the team.

- Steps that require collaboration of multiple team members are best kicked off around a whiteboard. Use the step planning template included in this chapter. The goal is to create a shared understanding of the Why and What.

- Throughout the step, the sub-team working on it (AKA step force) will collaborate, and essentially co-develop the requirements. Not all decisions have to come from the product manager or the designer.

- The step backlog can be translated into a Sprint/Kanban backlog for the team to execute. However, with Scrum it's best to keep the content of the sprint open to change to accommodate changes stemming from test results.

- Teams that use the GIST model transparently and objectively stand a better chance of gaining trust and decision delegation. It's best that managers and stakeholders are heavily involved in setting team goals, but allow the team to evaluate and test ideas in the order that it chooses.

- Using the four layers of GIST, and especially the Steps layer, helps break down the walls between product, business, and management, and lifts the fog around plans and product decisions.

Notes

[1] "User Story Mapping – Jeff Patton & Associates." https://www.jpattonassociates.com/user-story-mapping/. Accessed Jun. 1, 2020.

[2] Gothelf, Jeff and Josh Seiden. 2016. *Lean UX: Designing Great Products with Agile Teams*, O'Reilly Media, https://www.amazon.com/Lean-UX-Jeff-Gothelf-ebook/dp/B09BH8RF8M

CHAPTER 6

The Evidence-Guided Company

Now that we've explored the four parts of the GIST model it's time to zoom out to see how evidence-guided thinking is implemented at company level. We'll touch on strategy, large projects, dependencies, roadmaps, and other tricky topics.

To do all this I'll use an example: the semi-fictional company AcmeInvoice.ai (inspired by a number of companies I have worked with and observed).

The Story of AcmeInvoice

AcmeInvoice was one of the first companies to put machine learning in the service of invoice processing. As a startup, it discovered a big pain point within accounting firms that had to process piles of invoices and receipts submitted by clients in anything from crumpled, faded paper slips, to fuzzy mobile photos. The company forged ahead with a breakthrough solution that used a mobile app and cloud-based software to automate the Sisyphean task of parsing invoice data and entering it into the accounting system.

It was hard to gain a footing in the conservative and risk-averse accounting market, but AcmeInvoice iterated relentlessly over its technology, user experience, and business model. After 18 months not only did it have a handful of loyal and satisfied customers, but it had also found product/market fit and a scalable, repeatable business model. Investors were now falling all over themselves to invest in AcmeInvoice, and with the money came a phase of rapid growth, both in market footprint and in company size. After another intensive two years

AcmeInvoice was already a recognized brand name. The company had dozens of customers and more than 300 employees.

But here things took a turn for the worse. Having exploited the early adopters market, the company was now facing longer sales cycles with mainstream accounting firms. The slowdown in business growth caused concerns among investors. Pressure was put on the business teams to generate sales, which then translated into pressure on the product team to provide "deal-closing" features. At the same time the pace of development had slowed down perceivably as the software became complex and hard to maintain, The executive team of AcmeInvoice—bolstered by a number of former senior executives from big-name financial institutions—tried to boost results by introducing layers of process and middle management, but that only made things worse. By its seventh anniversary, the company that was once nimble, market-focused, and quick to react was no more. In its place stood a midsize company encumbered by processes, politics, and mistrust.

It's at this point that the company leaders decided to switch to a mode of operation that is evidence-guided, adaptive, and empowering. A manager who had used the GIST model in the past promoted it internally, and the executive team gave the green light to start using GIST in the product organization. The change was not immediate or easy, but within six months the improvement was clear. Product planning and execution had transformed from an arduous top-down, command-and-control exercise, back to the agile/lean mode of discovery that typified the company's early years. Managers and employees were brought closer together, and it was clear how the strategy was being turned into action. In the following year evidence-guided thinking had spread across the company, including to the business, operations, and executive teams.

We now join AcmeInvoice to see how it's operating on a regular basis.

Product Strategy

In the past AcmeInvoice's strategy consisted of a series of big ideas that resulted in long and expensive projects (big bets). One prominent example was the company's attempt to launch a software-as-a-service product targeted at small-to-medium accounting firms. The project took two years and thousands of person-weeks to develop, yet it yielded very few sales. In hindsight the company had neither a clear target market nor a good definition of what a "SaaS product" should do, which led to a do-it-all product that appealed to very few buyers. The product was eventually discontinued during an economic downturn and most of the team was laid off.

Today the leaders take a different approach to forming product strategy. They actively seek *strategic opportunities*—market segments with clear, strong needs, where the company can potentially step in and create high customer value and a viable business. Opportunities are identified through research—customer, competitive, market—but anyone in the company can float opportunities as they see them. The chief product officer collects the opportunities, vets them against the company's business strategy, and periodically reviews with the leadership team. When a promising opportunity is identified, it is assigned to a strategy squad, typically composed of experienced product managers, designers, researchers, engineers, and business folk. The strategy squad attempts to quickly size up and validate the opportunity through market research, competitive analysis, business modeling, customer interviews, surveys, and fake door tests. The findings are reported back within weeks to the executive team with recommendations.

Most opportunities turn out to be less meaningful than they first seem (as the company could have probably learned had it tried to validate its SaaS idea), but some yield clear supporting evidence. In these cases a nuclear product team may be created with a charter of discovering product ideas with strong product/market fit potential and high business upside. The team uses the GIST model: it defines measurable goals, generates and prioritizes ideas (which often requires further research), and validates them through steps. Typical steps at this stage include usability studies, Wizard of Oz tests, concierge tests, and early adopter programs (see my eBook in the companion page of this book for a refresher on these).

Most of these *Strategic Tracks*, as they are called in AcmeInvoice, fail to discover a product idea that ticks all the boxes—valuable, feasible, usable, and business-viable—and are eventually shut down. However, these are not considered losses but rather smart strategic bets that open up options for the company at a relatively low cost.

Using this process, AcmeInvoice eventually struck gold and found a massive opportunity in enterprise travel expense reporting. It turned out that a sizable portion of enterprises still use arcane ERP systems to collect and process employees' travel expenses. The experience is very poor both for the employees filing the expenses and for the finance teams processing them. These systems are old, brittle, and almost impossible to update. The Travel Expenses strategic track team was able to create in a matter of weeks a prototype based on AcmeInvoices's technology in which employees had only to take mobile phone photos of the receipts they got when traveling, and at the end of the trip a complete and correct expense report would be submitted on their behalf with a click of a button. The demo wowed CFOs and finance teams, and the team was able to sign eight companies to an early adopter program,[1] and a dozen more on a waiting list. The team was also able to create a compelling business case, where the company could sell the solution both to its core market of accounting firms, and directly to enterprises, creating exactly the engine of growth that the business strategy had called for.

Presented with this evidence the executive team decided to fund a larger project. But while optimistic, the managers knew full well that there's a big difference between producing a helpful prototype and promising projections, and launching a successful product. Committing a large team to build and sell an idea that hasn't yet found product/market fit (premature scaling) was the mistake they made with the SaaS project. To give this opportunity the best chance they formed a new Travel Expenses group composed of 13 engineers and a handful of product managers and designers, reporting to a trio of dedicated directors—product management, engineering, and design—who in turn report to the chief product officer. The end-of-year goal of this newly formed product group (aided by the rest of the company) is to develop a version of the product that showed clear evidence of product/market fit—namely to turn at least six of the eight early adopter clients into paying reference customers who were uploading expense invoices on a regular basis.

Top Metrics and Metrics Trees

In the past, AcmeInvoice's leadership team would routinely set targets for a long list of business key performance indicators (KPIs). The proliferation of KPIs made prioritization very hard—every product idea was somehow important and many decisions required a manager to intervene.

Today, the leaders focus the organization first and foremost on two top-level metrics:

- **North Star Metric**—*Number of documents processed per month (DPM).* Every document successfully parsed by the system is one less that a human has to handle and is therefore an increment of value for the customers.

- **Top Business Metric**—*Revenue.* As a private company, it's important for AcmeInvoice to grow gross revenue rapidly as a way to fuel further expansion and to attract investors on favorable terms.

Metrics Trees

Below the two top-level metrics, the company had mapped multiple levels of contributing submetrics. Creating the metrics graphs was a tough, but important exercise. It helped model growth and showed where the company is underperforming.

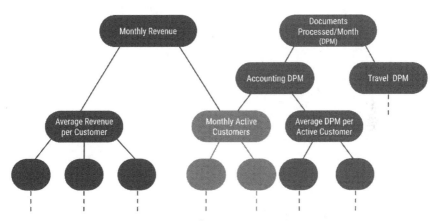

FIGURE 6.1: Top of AcmeInvoice's metrics tree

This year the leadership team introduced a slight update to the metrics graph by breaking the North Star Metric—documents processed per month (DPM)—into *Accounting DPM*, representing the company's core product, and *Travel DPM*, representing the new Travel Expenses strategic direction. It's not expected that Travel DPM will contribute much, but the leaders wish to set targets for it as a way to measure progress and to signal to the rest of the company that this metric is of high importance. Revenue isn't broken down into Accounting and Travel submetrics yet, because this year there's no revenue target for the Travel Expenses product. The true business metric the group is committing to is the number of active customers by end of year. In the following years as the product matures, it's likely to have revenue targets as well. In the long run, if the two products turn into separate business units, the company may choose to create metrics trees for each, potentially with different North Star Metrics and Top Business Metrics.

Apart from these metric graphs, the company is also tracking a number of health metrics that measure the health of the products, the business, and the company. Among those are average customer satisfaction, average employee satisfaction, and the company's overall carbon footprint.

Company Goals

With the strategy and metrics in place, the company's leaders have most of the building blocks they need to define goals. Company-level goals, captured in Objectives and Key Results (OKR), are set for a full calendar year and reviewed, and sometimes updated, at the end of each quarter.

This year the executives have chosen to focus the company on three objectives.

Yearly Company OKRs

- **O: Intelligent invoice Processing That Accounting Firms Love**

  - KR: Grow average number of documents processed per month from 25,000 to 38,000

  - KR: Grow yearly revenue from $120MM to $175MM

  - KR: Service availability up from 98.7% last year to 99.9%

  - KR: Security: 100% of users protected from latest fraud and ransomware attacks

  - KR: New markets: At least 10 new, large customers signed up in India, Brazil, and Southeast Asia

  Context: _Why these goals?_

- **O: Find Product/Market Fit in Enterprise Travel Expenses Processing**
  - KR: At least 6 enterprise paying customers using AcmeInvoice for travel expenses processing with at least 20 employees each
  - KR: At least 200 travel expenses per month processed via the new product

  Context: Enterprise travel expenses processing is a very big opportunity for us. The evidence suggests a very big need, that our document processing capabilities are a great match for. This year we need to discover a product that fits that needs very well and is also business-viable. Read more

- **O: Continuously Improve AcmeInvoice to be Modern, Efficient, and a Great Place to Work**
  (*Why this goal?*)
  - KR: Reduce time spent in meetings from 14% to 8%
  - KR: Employee aggregate satisfaction score of 4.7/5.0 (up from 4.3/5.0 last year)
  - KR: Move to ___ product launches per week (up from one per 1.5 week on average now)
  - KR: _____
  - KR: _____

  Context: We've made major progress in the last 18 months on all fronts. Employee and manager surveys indicate that the company is now much more focused, and agile; job satisfaction has risen significantly, but our self-improvement must continue and we still have some gaps to close. Read more

These Company OKRs may seem embarrassingly sparse, especially compared to the dozen or more OKRs AcmeInvoice managers used to create prior to adopting Evidence-Guided thinking, but experience has shown that this is just the right amount of detail to drive strong focus and achievement.

The first OKR has to do with the core product the company sells to accounting firms. The key results include targets for the two top metrics, improvement in service availability and security, and international expansion. All stated as outcomes rather than initiatives or projects (output). Is this all the company will have to do with its flagship product this year? Absolutely not, but company goals are not meant to sum up all the work, or even all the outcomes. The purpose of the goals is to specify where the company wants to be by the end of the year, and only the most important achievements at that. Other outcomes will be captured in lower-level goals, and most day-to-day work will be taken care of without a specific goal.

The second OKR is about the company's strategic move into the area or enterprise travel expenses. It is short on key results—essentially just two metrics that define what product/market fit means in this case—but long on context. The leaders wish to communicate why this opportunity was chosen and why it is important. The new Travel group will depend on other teams' help, so it's important to send the message clearly that this is a top priority for the company. Like in the other OKR clusters, there's a link to an outside document that provides yet more context: reasoning, evidence, and analysis. AcmeInvoice's leadership wants people to be in the know and is not worried about exposing too much or having its decisions scrutinized.

The last OKR is about the self-improvement of the company itself. AcmeInvoice has gone through a successful transformation, but the leadership team wants to keep improving. Some values and key results are missing. This is a draft, and the leaders ask for suggestions from middle managers and teams in order to complete the OKR.

The Product Organization: Structure and Goals

The product organization that includes engineering, user experience, product management, user research, and data analytics has three layers of leadership: product teams, product groups, and overall product org.

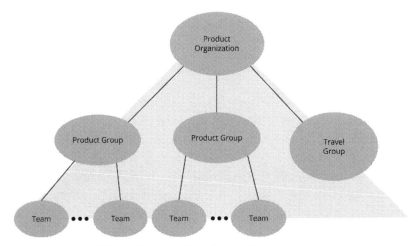

FIGURE 6.2: Structure of AcmeInvoice's Product organization

Product Teams

The company has adopted a model of *team empowerment*[2] that strives to distribute knowledge and decision-making. For this reason the product org is made up of a dozen product teams, each with its own area of responsibility and mission. Product teams are made up of up to ten engineers, a product manager, and a UX designer (some PMs and designers work with more than one team; some technology teams don't have a designer). The team is led by the *Team leads*: a trio of PM, designer, and engineering tech lead. The leads aren't directly managing any of the team members, but they are responsible for steering the team.

Product teams are expected to develop expertise in their area of work: technology, product, users, market, business, and so on. Thus, the company is trying to keep the org structure relatively stable and avoid the yearly re-org that it used to practice in the past. In keeping with the GIST model, each team has its own goals and manages its own idea bank.

There are three types of product teams:

• Functional area teams—These teams develop products and features used by external users and specialize in a particular part of the product. For example: Invoice ingestion, Invoice Processing, ERP system integration, and Reporting.

- Platform/Service/Technology teams—These teams develop systems and technologies to be used by other product teams or by other internal customers. For example Machine learning, Dev tools, and Backend Services.

- Ad hoc teams—Important goals that don't map nicely to the organizational structure sometimes require creating temporary teams with representatives from across the org. These teams typically operate for a few quarters, and members' work may be part-time. We saw one example already in strategy squads that validate strategic opportunities, strategic track teams that seek strategic ideas within an opportunity. Another example came during the first year of the company's transformation toward an evidence-guided way of work, where a cross-functional team of senior employees helped steer the change.

Product Groups

Product teams are aggregated into Product Groups of up to five teams. In AcmeInvoice this grouping is done by customer type. There's a group specializing in accounting firms, one who's focused on the clients of the accounting firms, and one that is developing tools and technologies for the use of the other teams (internal customers). The grouping brings together teams that are likely to work together, but there's also a lot of collaboration across groups, so the grouping is considered somewhat arbitrary. For this reason there are no group-level OKRs.

Groups are managed by a trio of director-level managers: product management, engineering, and UX. Group directors play an important role in "connecting the dots" and ensuring that teams have the bigger picture in mind. They identify areas of overlap or conflict between teams and ensure joint work toward the company's goals, strategy, and mission. Group directors regularly review team work (for example OKRs, the GIST board, and current steps) and provide feedback and recommendations or ask for improvements. They let teams make their own decisions, yet ensure that these decisions are backed by good evidence and reasoning. Group leaders also help remove obstacles, acquire funding and resources, and amplify the voice of the teams and of individual contributors to management. Group leaders have a broad view of the technology, product, market, and business, and are therefore often in a good position to identify opportunities, risks, and promising ideas.

The newly formed Travel group is a special case. The entire group is working together in "startup mode" (everyone is doing whatever it takes) so there are still no clearly defined product teams. In this case the group leaders set the goals for the entire group. If the product proves successful, the group will grow and split into product teams, each with its own area of responsibility and goals.

Product Org Management

The entire product organization is co-led by another trio: the Chief Product Officer, Chief Technology Officer, and Head of Design. Their collective mission is to ensure that the product org is working smoothly and efficiently toward achieving the company's goals. They ensure that the teams have the funding, head count, context, and tools they need to do their jobs. They also continuously work to facilitate cross-functional collaboration. For this reason there are no separate OKRs for Product Management, Design, or Engineering (disciplinary goals). AcmeInvoice had plenty of those in the past, but they proved to do more harm than good, pulling people in different directions and making it hard to collaborate.

Collaboration also extends outside the product organization. The heads of the product organization collaborate closely with the heads of Sales, Marketing, Legal, Finance, and other departments. Similarly the group leads and team leads keep close ties with their peers in these other departments. To ensure strong alignment between the work of the product organization and the goals of the company, engineering or design-specific goals are few, and are embedded in the company OKRs. We saw examples in the company OKRs earlier, with key results to do with improving security, availability, and launch frequency.

Managing Ideas

In the past, AcmeInvoice spent much time prioritizing ideas and planning roadmaps. There was contention over which ideas to choose, and the discussion was rife with debate and politics. Invariably, most of the resources were invested in big ideas coming from management, and "deal-closing" ideas coming from the field. The product org didn't have much of a say on these business decisions, but in turn had occasionally introduced big engineering and design projects that took years to complete. The results were consistently underwhelming, and it became evident that the company was wasting time and resources on the wrong things. Over time confidence in the leadership teams' ability to choose the right ideas had waned.

Today, AcmeInvoice makes a conscious effort to reach broad consensus and alignment on *goals*, but push product idea collection and prioritization to the teams. Each product team has its own idea bank, typically managed by the product manager, but open to anyone to review and to propose new ideas (by talking to the product manager who manages the bank).

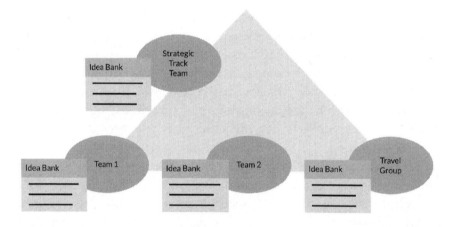

FIGURE 6.3: Idea management

In the idea bank, ideas are ranked by ICE score. Impact is generally calculated with respect to the company's North Star Metric—number of documents processed. There are a few exceptions: the Conversions and Billing team measures impact on the Top Business Metric—revenue— and the Platform teams, which build internal tools, technologies, and services, measure impact by the amount of usage their software gets.

At the AcmeInvoice of the past, Impact and Ease/Cost were part of the discussion, but the estimates were based on opinions, intuition, and sparse customer feedback. This is how the SaaS idea and many others had made the cut. The introduction of the third element of

ICE—Confidence—in conjunction with the Confidence Meter (see Chapter 3) changed the dynamics. Now people routinely ask, "What's the evidence?" even for ideas coming from the CEO, and say things like, "We have anecdotal evidence" or "This is backed by market data." The hype, salesmanship, and pressure tactics had been defused, and now, idea prioritization discussions are shorter and more concrete.

Big Ideas and Inter-Team Dependencies

The company recognizes that some big ideas will span more than one team, but it practices the mantra of *think big, but start small* (copied from early Google). We've already seen one example—the Travel Expense idea that came out of the company strategy discovery process has gradually grown in size and investment as stronger evidence was found.

A similar approach can take place at team level or group level. A product team may discover (or be handed) an idea that promises to bring about high impact. Such ideas typically take months or quarters to implement, and they often depend on other teams' collaboration. Still the team can choose to validate the idea in cheap ways (the *Assessment* and *Fact-Finding* techniques I describe in Chapter 4), and if supporting evidence emerges, ask for approval to invest more. The decision lies with the group managers; they can approve pursuing a very promising idea further through early-stage and mid-stage testing techniques. If these yield evidence that the idea is strong, the green light may be given to go all-in, and other teams may be invited to join. In other words, AcmeInvoice isn't averse to big ideas, but it wishes them to grow organically as the level of confidence in the idea grows. This is exactly what happened in the Tabbed Inbox project I told you about in Chapter 1; it started as a local initiative of one team within the Gmail Desktop group, and gradually grew to a large project that touched almost every part of Gmail.

As big ideas grow into larger projects that multiple teams work on in concert, more coordination and project management is required. However, at this point the idea has been tested and iterated on, and most of the functional, usability, and technical questions have been answered. There's far little need for big-room planning and specification, the banes of large projects AcmeInvoice undertook in the past. The teams mostly collaborate on delivery of a well-understood and mostly-specified product idea.

A related topic is one of inter-team dependencies. In the past, product teams were severely limited in the ideas they could pursue because execution often depended on other teams. This problem hasn't entirely gone away (and likely never will), but the company was able to reduce its severity by employing these principles:

- Strategic alignment—With the company leadership producing fewer, more focused OKRs, and with the introduction of the North Star Metric and Top Business Metric, the teams became much more aligned on what they were trying to achieve. The practice of *Shared OKRs* (covered in Chapter 2) and the facilitation of middle managers further help teams to enlist each other's help and collaborate on highest-impact ideas.

- Tactical independence—The product org's leaders iterated on team topology to try and reach a state where each team would have both a clear area of ownership and most of the resources it needed to act. One of the considerations is when to move expertise or resources (for example machine learning, or backend experts) into a separate Platforms and Services team. The managers realize that these moves, while theoretically improving resource efficiency, are also creating new dependencies.

Managing the Work: Steps, Tasks, and the GIST Board

AcmeInvoice's engineering teams use Scrum. In the past, a lot of effort went into planning the two-week sprints. It was expected that the product managers and designers would complete all specification and design work up front, so the team would be able to assess exactly how much work is included and to move swiftly into coding. Once a sprint was started, changing scope or requirements was strictly prohibited. This, in essence, pushed the product team to work in a mini-waterfall mode. Delivering product backlogs, user stories, mockups, and working code to the next in line became the goal. Despite all the hard work, new software launched to the market very slowly and rarely satisfied customers and stakeholders.

Today, AcmeInvoice makes it a priority that product teams will focus not just on tasks, but also on the top three levels of the GIST stack: goals, ideas, and steps. Each team maintains its own GIST board that captures the goals, ideas, and steps the team is working on now. Each team meets every other week for 30 minutes to go over the board. During the meetings, team members review progress on goals, whether they're pursuing the best ideas, and status of active steps.

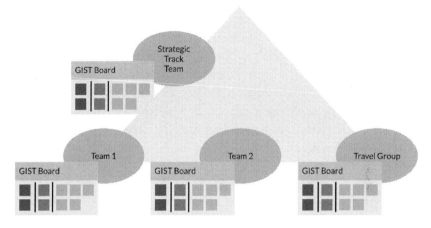

FIGURE 6.4: Every team manages its own GIST board

Immediately after the GIST board meeting the teams plan their next sprint, but the rules are much more relaxed. The engineers get a lot of context from the GIST boards, and are closely involved in the planning of individual steps, so they no longer need detailed requirements and user stories. Throughout the sprint they work with the PM and the designer to define and iterate on the behavior and interfaces. Detailed tickets were replaced by high-level 1-pagers and low-fidelity mockups. The strict demands for immutable sprint scope have also been dropped, as they limit teams' ability to react to new information. This change goes hand in hand with a change in performance measurement. No one measures team progress by the number of tickets or story points delivered any more. Team success is measured by its ability to achieve its goals as stated in the OKRs. If a team falls short it is encouraged to use retrospectives, five-why analyses, and continuous improvement goals. One might say that this mode of work is truly agile.

GIST boards are implemented using Google Sheets and are visible to everyone in the company. In fact, it's common practice to look at a team's GIST board as a way to learn what it is working on. Still, the PMs make a point of sharing snapshots of their GIST boards bi-weekly, and managers and stakeholders are encouraged to review those and send questions and feedback. Periodically, product teams may be asked to present their status to the heads of the product org, or even to the executive team. They will use their OKR doc, idea bank, and GIST board to support their presentation. Strategic track teams that work to discover strategic ideas within an opportunity also keep a GIST board and hold similar reviews with the CPO and the executive team.

Managing OKRs, ideas banks, and GIST boards definitely incurs process overhead, especially on the product managers. However, the extra load is balanced by the reduction in specification overhead. Overall it's a tradeoff the product managers are happy to make as they feel that they're achieving more, collaborating more closely with their colleagues, and generally having more impact and more fun.

The Roadmap

I mentioned AcmeInvoice's past devotion to yearly roadmaps. Though time-consuming and hard to do, planning the major product launches for the entire year was considered imperative. Head count, funding, and business projections were all based off the roadmap. The roadmaps were also seen as a sales tool of sorts, informing customers of what's coming and reassuring them that their favorite features are in the plan.

But there were obvious problems. For one thing, execution rarely followed the plan. Projects regularly slipped by months or even quarters, which reduced managers' and stakeholders' trust in the product org. On the other hand, executives regularly reshuffled the roadmap with new priorities and strategic directions, which caused much waste and made the product organization skeptical of the plans. Perhaps worse, the roadmaps didn't seem to affect the company's business performance in any meaningful way—most of the revenue and usage still came from products and features that were developed years ago.

In candid discussions, company leaders eventually acknowledged that the roadmap process was not working. They agreed that it's better to sacrifice (seeming) predictability in favor of actual results. Output roadmaps were put to rest, and in their place *Outcome Roadmaps* were brought in. Here's an example of the yearly roadmap the company is using now:

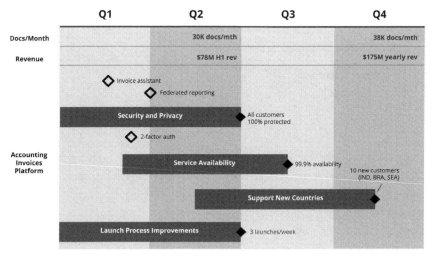

FIGURE 6.5: Outcome Roadmap

This roadmap reflects the company's yearly objectives and key results. At the top you can see the expected growth in North Star Metric and Top Business Metric. Below, the full diamonds represent specific key results and their target completion dates. The orange bars indicate periods of activity leading to these key results. You can see that work on beefing up Security will commence at the beginning of the year, but the efforts toward launching new countries will start only in mid-Q2. These timings are chosen based on head count, budgets, seasonal sales cycles, and other factors. Scheduling outcomes on a timeline and allocating resources toward achieving them were new skills AcmeInvoice had to develop. Just like with classic roadmaps it's part guesswork, part science, and in hindsight the accuracy isn't any worse, which means that outcome roadmaps can slip too.

You may have noticed that the outcome roadmap also includes some outputs. The hollow diamonds, for example Invoice assistant, and 2-Factor authentication, represent specific feature ideas. These ideas have been sufficiently validated so there's good reason to believe that they will contribute to the outcomes. The teams responsible for them are now working on delivery. There's no reason not to share such launches on the roadmap, and more will appear over time as other ideas are validated. For those interested in what's in the pipeline, the product org shares the list of candidate ideas, with their confidence levels, for each of the company goals. For example:

Security: 100% of users protected from latest fraud and ransomware attacks
- **2-Factor Authentication** (High confidence) ETA: 15 March
- **P-auth support** (Medium confidence)
- **Security Audits** (Low confidence)

Obviously this list is volatile as ideas come and go, hence it's not part of the OKRs or the roadmap. Still, it is very useful for the customer-facing teams to get this information. The confidence level is a good indicator of which ideas they should actively work on and which to just keep on their radar.

When the outcome roadmap was first proposed, everyone expected Marketing and Sales to push back. However, it turned out that both departments were unhappy with the old roadmap process as well, and were open to trying out a more adaptive way of working. For the Marketing team, this meant withholding time-consuming work on product ideas until they gained at least medium confidence. Likewise, the Sales team adapted to the lack of certainty in product launches. Customers demanding specific features, or a detailed launch roadmap, were invited to meet with a product manager who would capture the need underlying the requests and see how they correlated with the outcome roadmap. Sometimes the message was "We're working exactly on this problem. We're trying out a few things, but this is expected to land in Q3." Other times the customer input would be taken in, discussed, and at times cause a change in goals and plans. What the business teams lost in perceived predictability they more than gained in having a product organization that is truly working toward business goals. In turn the Sales and Marketing are now helping the product teams find evidence and validate ideas, for example by conducting market research and forming early adopter programs. Pressure tactics and escalations have gone down dramatically.

Another concern was that dropping development deadlines will hurt launch velocity and throughput (i.e. the developers will just take it easy). In hindsight the opposite turned out to be true. The removal of the big, must-have projects allowed the teams to become truly agile. The short cycles of steps meant there was less room for scope-creep, procrastination, and over-engineering. Achieving concrete user and business goals motivated engineers and designers much more than delivery deadlines (that no one believed in anyway). In hindsight there was no measurable drop in the number of features delivered, but there was a massive boost in outcomes.

The outcome roadmap turned into an important leadership tool. It made executives' expectations more concrete and it aligned teams and departments who collaborate on "shipping the roadmap" (as opposed to the output roadmap that was all the responsibility of the product organization). The roadmap helped affirm that the leaders truly prioritize outcomes over output and are serious about changing the way the company works.

Evidence-Guidance in Your Company

So much for AcmeInvoice and its use of evidence-guided thinking. Should you use exactly the process I have described above? Not necessarily. It's just an illustration of how one midsize company might use the principles and models covered in this book. While this is a B2B company selling to enterprise customers, of course the evidence-guided mindset applies also to business-to-consumer, multi-sided marketplaces, and other types of companies. The key is to adapt the processes to fit your reality, while maintaining the principles and frameworks intact. We will see how to do that in the next two chapters, *Scaling GIST* and *GIST Patterns*.

AcmeInvoice is somewhat of an extreme example—a company that went all-in on evidence-guided thinking. For many companies getting to this level of implementation would represent a very big change. It's important to understand you can gain benefits even if you don't do it all. In fact it's better if you don't try to change everything all at the same time. I'll show you in Chapter 9, Adopting GIST, where to start, and how to make progress.

Takeaways

- This chapter covers an example of how a midsize B2B company has implemented evidence-guided principles across the board, but this is by no means the only way to do it.

- Product strategy should not be a "roadmap on steroids" of big product ideas. Rather it's best to look for strategic opportunities (typically a market segment with strong underserved needs), then validate the most promising ones quickly through market research, competitive analysis, business modeling, customer interviews, surveys, and fake door tests.

- Validated opportunities can be turned into *Strategic Tracks*— Nuclear teams that seek meaningful ways to capture the opportunity. The strategic track team sets goals, does research, generates product ideas and validates them. Most tracks fail to find a way to capture the opportunity that ticks all the boxes, but with persistence the company may find potential winning ideas, that with more investment, may be developed toward product/market fit and a clear business model.

- Top-level metrics—The North Star Metric and the Top Business Metric—with their associated metrics trees help the leaders communicate what's most important to the company, set goals, and demonstrate how value capture and value delivery are tied together.

- Company-level OKRs should be set yearly and reflect strategic decisions as to what the company is trying to achieve by the end of the year. Fewer goals are better. The leaders should try to infuse the OKRs with context.

- In the *empowered product team* model, each cross-functional team has its own area of responsibility and is expected to develop expertise in product, technology, market, and user needs. Each team is led by a trio of Eng-lead, PM, and UX designer (if the team has one).

- Service and Platform teams have the same structure, but they focus on internal customers. From time to time the managers may decide to create an ad hoc team for a number of quarters to tackle specific cross-org goals or orgs that don't map well to the current org structure.

- The trio model is repeated at various levels of management in the product org, up to the CPO, CTO, and Head of Design.

- Mid-level managers have an important role assisting product teams and keeping them honest, communicating information both ways, aligning teams, and detecting opportunities, risks, and strong ideas.

- Each product team manages goals, ideas, steps, and tasks in its area of responsibility. It's recommended that teams keep OKRs, idea banks, and GIST boards visible to the entire company. These are also important tools during managerial reviews.

- From time to time the company may choose to follow big ideas that span teams. These ideas can come from the executive team, from middle management, or from the teams themselves. In all cases the trick is to start small, validating the idea in cheap ways, and then invest more based on the evidence.

- It's recommended to replace output roadmaps that lock the company into a plan, with outcome roadmaps that list when goals will be achieved on a timeline. Ideas that have been validated sufficiently can appear as deliverables on the roadmap. Ideas for which there isn't full confidence can be communicated with their confidence levels.

- The outcome roadmap requires an adjustment in how we level resources and plan work, and in what we communicate externally. What the business teams lose in (perceived) predictability they should more than gain in stronger collaboration with the product org and meaningful business impact.

Notes

[1] Early adopter programs involve testing a rough version of the product (think Alpha) with a small number of design-partners who represent the target audience and are willing to work closely with the product team on shaping the product. For more details see the eBook included in the companion page of this book.

[2] Made famous by Marty Cagan: https://www.svpg.com/empowered-product-teams/

CHAPTER 7

Scaling GIST

If you've made it this far, you may be considering adopting evidence-guided thinking and the GIST model in your company. But is GIST really right for your type of organization? Can it really work well with your own unique situation?

I'll try to answer these questions in the next two chapters. In this chapter we'll see how GIST works in companies of different sizes, from startups to enterprises. In Chapter 8, we'll talk about GIST in companies building products for enterprises, consumers, and SMBs, internal platform/services teams, multi-sided marketplaces, and physical products.

Let's start by seeing how to scale or shrink GIST to the size of your company.

GIST in Startups and Small Businesses

Startups, more than any other type of company, have to contend with high levels of uncertainty and risk. They need to execute and learn at breakneck speeds, while having very constrained budgets and often inexperienced leaders. In my experience, a lightweight use of GIST can create the necessary structure to drive the startup forward at high speed without burning through cash.

Goals

Goals should keep your startup laser-focused on what you need to do to survive and grow. Broadly speaking, there are two goals, often in this order:

- Find product/market fit
- Find a repeatable, scalable and profitable business model

GOALS FOR FINDING PRODUCT/MARKET FIT

Product/market fit (PMF) refers to a state in which a large (or growing) market segment with strong underserved need meets a "good-enough product."[1] According to the theory, product/market fit is a pivotal point in the life of the company. When customers are hungry for a solution, they will accept a less-than-perfect product from an unknown company without much pushing. In fact, they may "pull" the product out of your hands, leading to strong demand.

Finding product/market fit is therefore the objective. What would be the key results? One popular way to determine whether or not you have achieved PMF is the *Sean Ellis survey*[2] that measures customer sentiment based on the answer to the question, "How would you feel if you could no longer use the product?" Even stronger indications come from product metrics. These will depend on the type of product, market, and business model. Here are a couple of examples:

GOALS FOR A CONSUMER PRODUCT
(Inspired by growth expert and investor Andrew Chen):[3]

- Objective: Help enthusiast home cooks up-level their skills
  - KR: 6,000 lessons completed/week (the North Star Metric)
  - KR: 2,000 weekly active learners
  - KR: 30d retention > 20%
  - KR: At least 100 organic signups/week
  - KR: Estimated addressable market size > 50M users

GOALS FOR A PRODUCT SOLD TO MEDIUM OR LARGE COMPANIES

(inspired by serial entrepreneur and investor Christoph Janz):[4]

- Objective: Create the perfect solution for company-internal webpages and news
  - KR: 1000 new documents created per month (the North Star Metric)
  - KR: At least 6 customers using the product, with 10+ internal active users each
  - KR: Lead conversion rate of 25% or more
  - KR: Sales cycle of 4 months or less
  - KR: Estimated addressable market size of 300,000 seats or more

As you can see, these are big, audacious goals that should send a cold shiver down the spine of any entrepreneur. Still, these are the things you need to achieve, and stating them as goals will align founders, teams, and investors, as well as provide a way to measure *real* progress.

You'll need only this one OKR for the entire company. However, the usual three-month OKR cycle is too long for most early-stage startups. Many startups work in shorter time boxes of three to eight weeks, trying to make progress on one or two key results (or their submetrics) in each.

The North Star Metric may not be immediately clear as the startup is discovering how it will deliver value and to which market. In the book *Running Lean* entrepreneur and startup adviser Ash Maurya suggests that before finding product/market fit, the startup needs to detect a strong need and viable and feasible solution that addresses this need, a state he calls *problem/solution fit.*[5] At this early stage it's best to measure *customer traction*—the number of customers that are willing to make a commitment: signing up to your waitlist (B2C), agreeing to follow up meetings (B2B), agreeing to a pilot, and installing and starting to use your early product. After finding problem/solution fit, active users/customers can be a good fallback metric until you're ready to set your NSM.

What about the Top Business Metric? It's often counterproductive to set revenue or profit targets before you achieve PMF or even know what market you're targeting. In reality, the business metric you should care about the most is your *runway*—how long you have left to operate before running out of cash.

GOALS FOR FINDING A PROFITABLE, REPEATABLE, AND SCALABLE BUSINESS MODEL

There's no shortage of examples of startups that found product/market fit but could not create viable businesses (the dot-com boom and bust was full of them). To move to the next level of funding and growth, you'll need to also find a business model that shows you're ready to scale. According to investor and entrepreneur David Skok,[6] you should develop a business model that is:

- Repeatable—You have a process of acquiring and onboarding customers and users at a more or less fixed cost.

- Scalable—Investing 10x more money in acquiring and onboarding users will generate 10x more happy customers/users or an even greater number.

- Profitable—The cost of acquiring a customer is significantly lower than the lifetime value a customer will create.

This is a very challenging goal that can take years to achieve.

North Star Metric—At this point, you should know how you create value for your users and customers, and you should be able to choose a North Star Metric that measures the total value delivered.

Top Business Metric—Depending on your business model, you can consider a few options:

- Number of paying customers

- Total revenue

- Revenue by new customers or by expansion of old customers

- Monthly or annual recurring revenue (MRR/ARR)

- Remaining runway, if you're unsure what your business model is

Objectives and Key Results

It's likely that you now have the kernel of teams—product, sales, marketing. It's best to avoid the temptation to create separate sales, marketing, and engineering goals, and try to unite the entire company under as few goals as possible.

The metrics that indicate you've found the right business model depend on the type of product and the distribution channels. A SaaS company selling online should look at unit economics; for a direct-sales org, you'll care about the cost of acquiring and retaining a sales rep, the money she'll bring in, and her onboarding time.

Here's an example of an OKR for a SaaS company:

- O: Find a repeatable, scalable, and profitable growth model
  - KR: Cost of customer acquisition (CAC) < $20
  - KR: Customer Lifetime Value (LTV) > $75
  - KR: CAC payback time – 6 months or less
  - KR: 14d retention > 50%
  - KR: Churn rate < 2.5%/month

It may sound like this phase is all about the business side of the company, however, the product team too will have its hands full deepening product/market fit and reaching the levels of retention/churn required by the business model. The initial product you've built is likely full of shortcuts and gaping holes that were fine for early adopters, but may prevent you from moving forward with other customers. It's good to set key results for closing those as well.

Ideas

Startups are often formed on the basis of one big idea. However, even if the founders are experts in the field, it's very unlikely that this exact idea will succeed. Nevertheless, some entrepreneurs choose to go all-in on their big idea without much consideration for other options. Other founders try to do it all at the same time, or pivot from one idea to the next at a high rate. Good idea prioritization can help strike a balance— keeping extreme focus, yet staying open to new options.

Prior to problem/solution fit, things are quite open-ended— anything could be considered a valid idea when you don't yet have a clear market and product. Having an idea bank, typically managed by the founder in charge of product management, can help. At this stage the idea bank should hold the possible products that the company may develop. Initially, there may be few ideas, but if we do our job right and conduct research and test these ideas, we will come up with other, often better ones.

After problem/solution fit the startup should have a high-level understanding of what it is going to develop (sometimes called a *product vision*), although pivots may still occur on the way to product/market fit. The idea bank will start filling with ideas for features within this bigger product vision.

In a startup, emotions run high and information is often scarce. You can evaluate ideas using ICE (Impact, Confidence, Ease) or another unbiased method to balance your judgment with evidence. There's usually a tension about what's Impact—the founders need to choose between following the vision or going after whatever gets customers to use and buy. There's no right answer. Sometimes the market will pull you toward a niche product that doesn't scale, other times listening to customers leads to surprising results. For example, early on the founders of Microsoft believed that personal computers Unix will be the future operating system of personal computers, and saw PC-DOS, which Microsoft developed as a contractor for IBM, as a stop-gap solution. However PC-DOS led to MS-DOS and later to Windows, the operating systems that powered almost all the world's PCs and that turned Microsoft into a software empire.

As the startup progresses toward product/market fit and a business model, business ideas will gradually be added—channels, partnership, pricing models, promotions. Initially, it's best to keep those in the same idea bank as they'll compete for the same scarce resources. This will help keep communication and alignment going even as teams start forming. Eventually, when the number of people and ideas grows larger, the idea bank will naturally split. When that time arrives, it's a good idea to split by goals rather than by disciplines or product areas.

Steps

Startups face very high levels of uncertainty. Testing ideas and hypotheses at high speed is crucial, both before and after finding product/market fit. It's important to resist the urge to go into a development frenzy aimed at launching v1.0 as early as possible. You are likely to waste development effort, time, and cash just to discover that you built the wrong product or that the business model you've chosen doesn't scale.

Prior to problem/solution fit, work will mostly involve research: customers observations and interviews, market and competitive research, and technology evaluation. Customer interviews are especially important to determine whether you're working on the right opportunity. As you identify key needs you can start testing ideas through early testing steps: usability tests, fake door tests, and concierge tests. When your confidence in specific ideas grows you can move into mid-stage testing, producing rough versions of your idea(s) that can be tested by the customers themselves (in the startup world these are often called Minimum Viable Product, or MVPs, although different people have different definitions of the term). Running through your build-measure-learn loops quickly is of crucial importance. The rate of learning is just as important, if not more, than the speed of development.

The AFTER framework we explored in Chapter 4: Assessment → Fact-Finding → Tests → Experiments → Release Results, can help you run through many ideas fast. Startupists who master the art of assessment and fact-finding can save a lot of time and effort by eliminating ideas that already prove weak on paper. It's also a good party trick to impress investors with.

Tasks

In a startup, everyone should take part in finding product/market fit and a viable business model. Hiring people just to code, create designs, or generate user stories is a massive waste. As we saw in Chapter 5, disconnect between managers and developers, and between business and product, can occur in startups too. Creating one GIST board as the key project management tool will keep the entire company in sync. The caveat is that the board will have to be updated very frequently as ideas and steps are defined at a high rate. As the startup grows, and the development teams start breaking into sub-teams, each will eventually have its own GIST board.

GIST in Scale-ups/Midsize Companies

Congratulations, you've made it through the hardest part. Finally, there's money to spend—investors are attracted to companies that can demonstrate product/market fit and growth potential. But along with the money comes an expectation of rapid growth, both in head count and in business results. This is a crucial—and risky—time of transition. With scaling come the realities of a bigger company, including middle management, specialized departments, more stakeholders, and complex dependencies. Newly hired execs bring their own playbooks from previous companies, and you may see a proliferation of departmental goals and processes—the beginning of siloing. It's harder to work at a high pace, yet there's no time for careful planning—everything is done in a rush.

Many companies lose their momentum at this stage, and some also lose customer focus and the ability to learn and innovate quickly. In Chapter 6, we saw a full example of how such a company can use GIST to rekindle the process of discovery and experimentation and to refocus on what really matters.

Goals

Alignment has never been more important than it is now. The company's leadership team should pick a clear North Star Metric that measures the amount of value we deliver to the market, and a Top Business Metric that we need to grow the fastest. Together with the company's top objective, or *mission*, these form the most important goal of the company. We should spare no efforts to communicate, then communicate again, this goal and align everything the company does around it. If there is a product vision and a strategy, those should be shared as well.

To make the top goal actionable and to drive alignment, it's important to identify submetrics and supplementary metrics (for example customer satisfaction, rate of system failure). There's a risk of losing yourself in the metrics, though. Leaders at every level should therefore establish meaningful missions/objectives for their area of responsibility.

At a midsize company, there should ideally be just two levels of OKRs: company level (planned yearly and reviewed quarterly) and team level (planned quarterly and reviewed every other week). Managers and employees should focus on defining a concise set of outcome goals, communicating top-down, bottom-up, and across with the facilitation of mid-level managers. Supplementary goals that fall outside the metrics trees should be part of the mix.

Pure departmental goals (for example marketing goals, engineering goals, and design team goals) should be discouraged or used sparingly as they can stand in the way of collaboration around the company's business and user goals (which are almost always cross-functional). Techniques like ad hoc virtual teams and shared OKRs should be put to use to facilitate cross-team and cross-department collaboration.

At this phase in the company, the desire for product roadmaps that show releases on a timeline may grow stronger. It's a good time to establish alternatives, such as the GIST outcome roadmap I presented in Chapter 6 that shows objectives, outcomes, and high-confidence ideas on a timeline.

Ideas

Idea contention grows considerably at this stage. With the growth in capital and human resources, managers may be tempted to invest in expensive, big-bet projects. Sales and marketing teams may ask for long lists of "must-have" features copied from competitors or requested by potential customers. Engineering and design may push for long-overdue redesigns of code and user interface. Growth teams may prefer to try out many small optimizations.

Hence, idea prioritization is of crucial importance. The goals you create every year and quarter will help drive focus and empower people to say No to things that fall outside the goals (or say Yes, being aware of the tradeoffs). Having clear owners and decision makers is also key, otherwise every idea will have to be debated by managers. This is a good time to define meaningful product teams with clear areas of ownership. There's never a perfect organizational topology, and you may have to iterate multiple times.

Each team should have its own idea bank which is ranked against one clear metric (ideally the company's NSM, or Top Business Metric; some teams will have idea banks for both). If you haven't already, it's a good idea to recruit product managers and establish product leader trios of PM/UX/Eng at every level. We want to start triaging ideas on a regular basis, factoring in evidence. ICE scoring can be very helpful for prioritization and for communication. Big ideas that span multiple teams should start small, first validated by a small sub-team, and gradually ramping up in head count and investment on the basis of evidence.

A midsize company that has only one money-making product is highly exposed to risk. It's a good time to start collecting and validating new strategic opportunities, generating strategic ideas that may take the company into new areas and diversify its product portfolio. These ideas should be managed in a separate bank, typically by a senior product manager. You can reuse the GIST startup playbook I detailed earlier— pursuing problem/solution fit, product/market fit, and a scalable business model as fast as possible.

Steps

As the product becomes more complex and development cycles grow larger, using the entire gamut of the AFTER model becomes very important. Many assumptions can be validated using Assessment, Fact-Finding, and early testing techniques, before committing engineering resources (and even then we should keep combining discovery and delivery).

The good news is that now there are many more potential and existing users to test with so you can use qualitative *and* quantitative methods of validation. It's a good time to bring in user researchers and data analysts and to establish a regular practice of user interviews, usability studies, field research, data deep dives, and A/B experiments. It's also crucial to give product teams direct access to customers and users, not mediated by protective layers of sales, customer support, and other customer-facing functions.

Tasks

With the higher level of stratification and the introduction of product managers, there's a risk your development teams will become less connected with customers and the business and increasingly focused on delivery. Using a GIST board and holding regular meetings to review and update it can be a good countermeasure. You should practice creating step backlogs, implemented by cross-functional step-forces and also have developers take part in user and market research. The GIST board will also become an important tool of communication with stakeholders, managers, and peer teams.

GIST in Enterprises

The defining characteristic of the enterprise is not just its size but the complexity of its structure. There may be divisions or business units, further split by product, market, or geography. There are central functions and regional offices. There are likely specialized departments (marketing, sales, finance, legal, finance, and so on), and platforms and services teams, which may be split across central, regional, and business units. The number of people with a stake in every decision grows significantly. There are also a lot more layers of management—a rank-and-file employee can be ten levels or more removed from the CEO.

As you are no longer able to know everyone personally, it is challenging to sustain trust in a large organization. Some of the symptoms of mistrust are top-down plans, restrictive processes, proliferation of output metrics and KPIs, lots of meetings (status, reviews, coordination), and senior managers having to be involved in minor decisions. Not surprisingly, many enterprises find that they are slow to move and almost unable to innovate. The business largely depends on products created years ago, as the company is unable to find another big win.

Addressing the woes of the enterprise is well beyond the scope of any one model. But it may be helpful to look at the principles that allow some large tech product companies to stay innovative. One of these principles is what Netflix calls being *highly aligned, but loosely coupled.* Here's how the company explains this concept in its Culture page:[7]

> *We avoid [becoming highly centralized and inflexible] by being highly aligned and loosely coupled. We spend lots of time debating strategy together, and then trust each other to execute on tactics without prior approvals. Often, two groups working on the same goals won't know of, or have approval over, their peer activities. If, later, the activities don't seem right, we have a candid discussion. We may find that the strategy was too vague or the tactics were not aligned with the agreed strategy. And we discuss generally how we can do better in the future.*

In other words, companies like Netflix avoid creating cascading plans for the entire organization and don't try to command-and-control the execution. Instead top leaders lead by setting a concrete strategy—an explanation of the markets in which the company wishes to operate and how it wishes to deliver and capture value—and by broadly explaining the context behind this strategy (called "leading with context" in Netflix).[8] Tactical decisions are pushed down to the right level, which could be middle management, or individual teams. Netflix fully expects mistakes to be made, but it's willing to pay this price and learn from these mistakes, rather than limit itself with restrictive planning-and-execution processes.

Not all companies are this forgiving. Apple and Amazon, for example, use similar strategy-led approaches, but expect product ideas to be reviewed and approved by managers, sometimes going all the way up the chain of command. In such companies managers are the deciders on many things; however, they are expected to decide based on evidence and analysis rather than just their opinions.

Another common pattern is to split the organization into business units or divisions built around concrete products areas (for example Android, or Alexa), which may split further into product-specific units. Each of these sub-divisions has its own product and business teams that work closely together and specialize in specific customers and markets. That means, for example, that each business unit can operate almost as a standalone medium-size company (and can potentially reuse the playbook we just saw earlier in the chapter), while the parent company acts somewhat like an investor that also offers central services such as recruiting, HR, and facilities. Company-wide strategy is again important to ensure that business units and individual products act in alignment, while retaining the ability to create their own strategy and tactics.

Goals

Goals are the power tool of the enterprise manager. Company executives use the goals to steer the ship, while allowing the organization to find the way.

North Star Metric—Some companies, for example Netflix or Meta, get by with just one North Star Metric. In other organizations, different parts of the company deliver value in different ways (for example Android vs. Google Chrome), so it makes sense to set the North Star Metric by business unit or even by product. The decision on what NSM to choose should be delegated to the people managing that product or business unit. Similarly, the metric trees are specific to a product or product area. For example, two products may have different meanings for *monthly active users*, and may put this metric higher or lower in their metrics trees.

Objectives and Key Results—In a large organization, in addition to having company-level OKRs and team-level OKRs, it makes sense to set OKRs for business units, products, or other meaningful nodes in the hierarchy. This will create an abundance of OKRs, so it's imperative to create at each level just the minimum set of objectives and key results. The leaders that create the OKRs should specify the goals within their scope, but be careful of setting their reporting teams' OKRs.

In enterprises, some company-level OKRs may be a copy of business-unit goals. That was the case in Google, where the company OKRs included OKRs taken from Chrome, Android, Geo, etc. But there may also be OKRs related to a strategy (for example to doubling down on expansion in emerging markets) or company-wide supplementary goals (for example reducing hiring biases.) As always, company-level goals should be re-visited, and perhaps adjusted, every quarter.

Ideas

If you've ever worked in a large company, you know how hard it can be to get your ideas through. One common antipattern are big top-down projects (AKA "big bets") that hog a lot of resources and often fail to generate positive results. I started this book by telling you about the multiyear Google+ project, but every large company has such stories. As a countermeasure we want to introduce the principle of *Think big, but start small*. Big projects have their place, but they are very risky. Such projects should stem from opportunities that are well backed by research, and should be based on ideas that have been thoroughly validated through multiple rounds of testing. The size of the project and the investment you're willing to put into it should be proportional to the level of confidence the idea enjoys (which of course should be based on evidence). Company leaders don't have the time or the skills to collect and evaluate opportunities and ideas. They can definitely suggest some, but it's best to delegate the validation to others and to make decisions based on the evidence they produce.

Some companies implement opportunity detection and idea incubation in dedicated *innovation labs* or internal *startup hubs* (good places to implement the startup playbook we saw earlier). Others hold these activities within the business units/product areas. Some companies encourage teams and individuals to devote some portion of their time to radical new ideas, and sometimes those lead to entirely new products (as was the case for the iPhone and Gmail). However, left alone, new products find it hard to compete with established products, and may be killed or crippled by business-line leaders. The company should therefore set goals for innovation and hold leaders at all levels accountable.

Even when your idea isn't competing against the latest big bet, it's still facing major challenges in an enterprise environment, including:

- Many dependencies—technical, operational, or other
- Strict conformance criteria and approvals
- Complex legacy products that are hard to change
- Large customer base that might be negatively affected by changes

These make developing an idea slow and expensive, which means you can take on fewer ideas—a very high price to pay. These are not easy things to fix, but solutions do exist. In the book *Lean Enterprise*,[9] Jez Humble, Joanne Molesky, and Barry O'Reilly describe how Amazon replaced its legacy monolithic architecture with a scalable service-oriented architecture (later the basis of Amazon Web Services) using the Strangler Fig pattern.[10] A later chapter tells the story of how Hewlett Packard's LaserJet Firmware team (400 people distributed across the USA, Brazil, and India) managed to revamp its development practices leading to an eightfold increase in the ratio of time devoted to innovation work. What's common to both these achievements is that they did not rely on a "big bang" project, but rather on years-long cycles of incremental improvements (which didn't block the company from launching new features and enhancements). Whatever the approach, you should make such improvements a priority.

As ideas become more expensive, good idea prioritization becomes paramount. Having a solid base of concise goals is very important, as is having a transparent and objective prioritization system such as ICE.

Each product team (aka squad) should manage its own idea bank. Cross-team ideas can often be managed by the teams using shared OKRs. When a big, new idea comes along, we should check if it's not better represented as a goal ("Allow users to socialize through our products" vs. "Build a new social network") or as an opportunity.

Steps and Tasks

As usual, our preference is to have semi-autonomous product teams manage their GIST boards that reflect the goals, ideas, and steps within their scope. As there are more dependencies between teams, some steps will require cross-team collaboration. Early-stage steps are rather short and minimal, so usually there's no need for big-room planning and elaborate project management. As ideas mature and more teams join the effort, late steps may take the form of managed projects, with more traditional project management. At this point, it's mostly about coordinated delivery of an idea we've already verified and have high confidence in.

Getting Specific

GIST works well for companies of different sizes and life stages, though the main value can vary. For startups, it's about keeping an intense focus on business goals (product/market fit, and later, business model) while rapidly experimenting, developing, and growing. For larger organizations, it's about keeping the spirit of product exploration going in an environment that is increasingly averse to ambiguity. In all cases, the model tries to keep your organization customer-focused, agile, evidence-guided, and team-empowering—the four principles that aid in dealing with uncertainty.

Still, these are generalizations. Company size is an important variable, but there are also the type of product and market to be considered. A company developing medical hardware is likely to have to use a different playbook from one developing a dating app, even if the two are of a similar size and life stage. In the next chapter, we will see how different types of organizations can adapt GIST to fit their specific needs.

Takeaways

- Startup goals focus the team on the most important achievements: first finding product/market fit and then establishing a scalable business model.

- Startups usually start with a very small set of ideas, but the list grows larger the more research and testing we do. It's best to keep just a single idea bank for the entire startup until a late stage.

- Startups need to learn fast and at very low cost. Using the AFTER model the founders will start by doing research, assessment, and fact-finding, then move to early-stage tests, before committing resources to build and test their ideas.

- Scale-ups/Midsize companies should use goals to align and focus the company at a time where there is much disorder and rapid growth. The North Start Metric, Top Business Metric, and their metrics trees are important tools at this stage for alignment and setting of priorities.

- Scale-ups/Midsize companies should establish product teams/squads with clear missions and areas of responsibility. The trio of team leaders (PM/UX/Eng) should set team goals, manage the idea bank, and create a GIST board.

- Principles such as "Strategically aligned, but loosely coupled" and "Think big, but start small" help some tech enterprises stay innovative and competitive despite their size and complexity. Having clear business units or product areas with their own dedicated product and business teams helps as well.

- Objectives and Key Results were created to help steer large companies. It's important to keep the OKRs as small as possible because there are so many of them across the org.

- Picking ideas to work on is very hard in an enterprise environment because of the contention with big-bet projects coming from the top. It's important to mitigate this by focusing on first detecting and validating opportunities and then testing ideas.

- Dependencies, legacy code and other factors may slow the rate of development in an enterprise and limit the number of ideas we can pick. It's important to set goals to mitigate these challenges (although ideally not through a big-bang project). At the same time good, transparent idea prioritization that factors in evidence becomes crucial.

Notes

[1] This article by Marc Andreessen has popularized the term product/market fit and explains it in full detail https://pmarchive.com/guide_to_startups_part4.html

[2] "Using Product/Market Fit to Drive Sustainable Growth." Apr. 5, 2019, https://blog.growthhackers.com/using-product-market-fit-to-drive-sustainable-growth-58e9124ee8db. Accessed Apr. 25, 2020.

[3] "Zero to Product/Market Fit (Presentation) – Andrew Chen." https://andrewchen.co/zero-to-productmarket-fit-presentation/. Accessed Jul. 9, 2020.

[4] "The Angel VC: WTF is PMF? (part 2 of 2) – Christoph Janz." Jul. 5, 2017, http://christophjanz.blogspot.com/2017/07/wtf-is-pmf-part-2-of-2.html. Accessed Jul. 9, 2020.

[5] Maurya, Ash. 2012. *Running Lean: Iterate From Plan A to a Plan that Works*, O'Reilly Media, https://leanstack.com/books/runninglean

[6] "The Most Important Startup Question—For Entrepreneurs." https://www.forentrepreneurs.com/most-important-startup-question/. Accessed Apr. 25, 2020.

[7] "Culture – Netflix Jobs." https://jobs.netflix.com/culture. Accessed Jul. 1, 2020.

[8] The book *No Rules Rule: Netflix and the Culture of Reinvention* by Reed Hastings, Erin Meyer, published by Penguin Press, offers a good overview of Netflix unique culture.

[9] Humble, Jez, Joanne Molesky, and Barry O'Reilly. 2015. *Lean Enterprise: How High Performance Organizations Innovate at Scale*, O'Reilly Media, https://www.oreilly.com/library/view/lean-enterprise/9781491946527/

[10] *Strangler Fig* is a pattern for migrating a legacy system by gradually moving pieces of functionality into new applications and services. It was first suggested by Martin Fowler and later explained in this 2004 paper by Stevenson, Pols et al. https://cdn.pols.co.uk/papers/agile-approach-to-legacy-systems.pdf

CHAPTER 8

GIST Patterns

The principles of setting user and business-focused goals, evaluating multiple product ideas, developing and testing ideas through Steps, and executing steps through team tasks are widely applicable. I've seen them being used to build casual games, multi-sided marketplaces, autonomous robots, enterprise-grade security, advertising platforms, and much more. Not all of these implementations are the same of course. There are important differences that have to do with the type of product, the market, and the business model.

In this chapter, I'll address these specifics. It's impossible to cover all the combinations of product, market, and business model, but I will try to touch on some of the most frequent ones in this chapter—both patterns and anti-patterns of using GIST.

GIST in Enterprise-Grade Products

If you're developing products for the enterprise market, chances are you feel somewhat skeptical or apprehensive about using methodologies like GIST. In my experience, the concerns revolve around the Ideas and Steps layers. Let's look at these more closely, one at a time.

Ideas

In many B2B companies, ideas are chosen based on what existing and potential customers are requesting. There's a good reason for that: sales cycles are long and hard, every acquired customer is a source of revenue for years, and losing a customer is very costly. Hence, gratifying customers is paramount, and the opinion of your Sales department, which handles most of the relationship with customers, weighs heavy.

Before we dive into how GIST addresses these needs, however, there are a couple of important underlying principles to touch on:

- **Product company vs. professional services company**—As executive and product coach Rich Mironov points out, "*Product companies build packaged, standardized products that they can sell many, many times to many, many customers with little or no customization—which lets them sell each unit for substantially less than it costs to build.*" In contrast, "*Professional services companies take on projects for individual clients, and price each engagement for profitability: cost plus 50% or 70% or 100% margin.*"[1] Repeatedly prioritizing one-off customer requests will slowly, but surely turn you into a professional services company that charges like a product company. It will also starve the product organization of the resources it needs to build a general-purpose product, and create a bloated codebase that is hard to maintain and improve on.

- **Product team vs. feature team vs. delivery team**—Product coach Marty Cagan made the distinction between these three approaches to product development: "*In an empowered product team, the product manager is explicitly responsible for ensuring value and (business) viability.*" In the other two models, however, "*the value and business viability are the responsibility of the stakeholder or executive that requested the feature on the roadmap. If they say they need you to build feature x, then they believe feature x will deliver some amount of value, and they believe that feature x is something that is viable for the business.*"[2] Large B2B product companies are especially prone to this line of thinking. As business teams and execs are in close touch with customers as part of the sales process, they believe they are fully capable of divining which product ideas are most important. However, that's just a sample of the market, and often not a representative one. Company requests tend to focus the company on the status quo and may miss big opportunities. For example both BlackBerry and Microsoft were dismissive of the iPhone as a business phone because it lacked two core "must-have" features that all business customers demanded: long battery life and a physical keyboard. But it turned out business customers were willing to let go of those features in favor of the benefits brought about by multi-touch smartphones. In the following years iOS and Android devices displaced both Microsoft-based and BlackBerry phones. Eventually BlackBerry lost so much market share that it had to shut down.

So, before you try to employ GIST, you need to tackle these two big questions: Do you want to work as a true product company (which still allows for the odd single-customer request as a rare exception)? And do you want to empower product teams to discover what products the market needs?

If the answer is yes to both, GIST may be right for your company, even if you're dealing with large, demanding customers. To demonstrate how, let's use an example. Assume a must-have request comes from your number one customer. According to the sales rep, the customer will surely drop us in favor of a competitor if we don't provide the desired feature.

Let's use ICE to evaluate this product idea:

- **Impact**—The questions we need to answer are: 1) If we build this feature, what growth will we see in our North Star Metric?, and 2) If we don't build it, what decline can we expect? We can use the sum of the absolute values of the two. Let's say that we estimate the feature will drive 5 percent growth in that single customer, but we don't believe anyone else will use it. That customer accounts for 20 percent of our monthly NSM, so it'll amount to 1 percent growth. On the negative side, if the customer drops us, we will be down 20 percent in our NSM. So, the total impact change is 21 percent, which is a solid 9 in our impact scale.

- **Ease**—After quick analysis, you estimate that it's going to be a midsize feature with ease of 5.

- **Confidence**—The Confidence Meter will indicate that what this idea has going is anecdotal evidence—a customer request—which is *low* confidence: 0.5 and change. The reason for the low score is that customers are not good at predicting their own future behavior.

They may change their mind and not use the must-have feature, keep changing the requirements, come up with other do-or-die features, take a long time to adopt, or even dump the product anyway—even if you provide everything they asked for. Having it all hang on one customer makes this a high-risk feature. Still, the rules of the game in enterprise are different. A single customer has more weight. So, some product teams adjust the weight and give anecdotal customer evidence coming from important customers a boost. Let's say in your company this makes the confidence a 2.

The total ICE score is therefore: 9 * 4.5 * 2 = 81. Now you have a basis of comparison with other ideas. Your stakeholders and managers may push back and say that NSM is all well and good, but they think in terms of revenue. You can do exactly the same exercise where impact is calculated on revenue per month. You can do it for this and other top ideas and then compare.

An important observation may come out of your ICE analysis: that this is a weak idea in absolute market value terms—its impact stems almost entirely from the threat of losing the customer. There should therefore be serious consideration whether the customer will really leave over this one feature or, conversely, if the customer will stay due to this feature. What other evidence do we have besides the word of the customer? How senior was the person making the threat? Are there other ways to gratify this customer? What's the underlying need that they have, and can we address it with a different feature that is maybe more broadly usable? Do they need the feature now or is it just something they wish to know will come one day? If the customer is threatening to walk away, how solid is the relationship? Are they otherwise satisfied?

In my experience, this discussion will lead to deeper investigation. The product manager may join a call with the customer. The CEO may have a chat with the customer's CIO. Pricing options may be discussed. As we collect additional evidence, a more nuanced picture will emerge. We may discover there are other, better options to help this customer, or that we should indeed build this product idea, or maybe that the customer has already decided to walk away and is just looking for an excuse. Whatever the outcome, ICE has made us evaluate the idea in an objective, rational way and may prevent us from making a costly mistake.

Steps

Enterprise product teams often feel that they're unable to use the principle of build-measure-learn. Many enterprise customers are slow to change and are averse to exposing their employees and business operations to anything but fully completed-and-tested products. Deployments are complex due to integration with customers' existing systems and may be subject to lengthy internal testing and validation. Often the product team does not have direct access to the customer or the internal users—everything is done through sales, customer support, customer success, or external integrators. Lastly, your company may be averse to the idea of testing with customers as the norm is to sell to them, support them, and then sell them some more.

All of this doesn't bode well for idea validation in an enterprise B2B company, and yet many are able to run steps and do it well. You can and should use validation steps in your enterprise projects. The speed will never be the same as with consumer or small-business products, but that's ok as long as you're learning faster than the competition. While every product and every customer is different, these validation techniques are almost always useful:

- **Interviews**—When selling to enterprises, quantitative data is usually scarce, and product adoption is complex, therefore, you should strive to talk to as many existing and potential customers as possible. For a big, new feature, aim for at least 15 interviews. For a new product, you should do even more. Pre-sale and post-sale meetings, product demos, and customer seminars are all great opportunities to interview customers, but don't rely solely on your sales pipeline to generate interviews. Conferences, LinkedIn, and (best) introductions are some good ways to get in touch with potential customers. Customer interviews are also a great way to create good leads for your early adopter program.

- **Early adopter programs**—Going into a lengthy sales cycle with a conservative customer is the antipattern of validation. The customer may drag you on for quarters—yielding very little actual learning—and eventually drop the deal. For a brand-new product idea, you'll need to find early adopter customers that will be willing to accept a less-than-perfect product and will help you shape the product to address their needs. In the book *Inspired*, Marty Cagan recommends finding six to eight reference customers, all from a single market segment. He advocates treating them as development partners—closely understanding their needs, communicating with high transparency, and avoiding selling them until the product is ready. According to Cagan, finding a product that meets the needs of these six to eight reference customers is equal to finding product/market fit in this market segment.

• **Data analysis**—In some cases, you'll have sufficient data from your existing customers to help build confidence in new ideas. Another rich source of insights is the customer relationship management (CRM) system, allowing you to analyze past customer engagements. I've seen PMs that leveraged these systems to add mandatory qualifying questions and even run value-proposition tests.

• **Concierge tests**—Concierge tests, where you and your teammates manually do what the software eventually will automate, are often the easiest first step to collaborating with large customers. They require very little commitment on the part of the customer, no integration effort, and can teach you an awful lot.

• **Pilots**—A pilot is often the first step to collaboration with a customer. Even customers that disagree with testing software on principle may agree to do a pilot. The allure of the pilot is that it confines the risks to a clear, well-defined area and it requires lower commitment on the part of the customer. During the pilot, you will have to fill a lot of gaps on behalf of the client. For example, if the product assumes that the customer will design a landing page through an external agency, guess what—you're the agency.

• **Don't rush to sell**—Few things are more disruptive for a company than sending a sales team with revenue targets to sell an as-yet-unvalidated product or feature. The product team will be distracted from product discovery and pulled into delivery commitments and sales support. The product will most likely fail to sell as it's yet to achieve product/market fit, creating a general sense of disappointment and mistrust. This does not mean that sales and marketing should be kept out of the loop during validation. It's best if a sales representative joins the cross-functional team and helps develop and validate the idea as well as the sales channel. This person, which Stanford Business management professors Mark Leslie and Charles A. Holloway call a "Renaissance Rep,"[3] (or may exist already in your company with the more old-fashioned title of business-development) will operate without sales quotas, marketing, or sales engineering support. She will help make the early adopter program succeed by finding potential reference customers, getting past hurdles and gatekeepers, taking care of contracts and terms, chasing the customers when they are not responsive, and eventually, when the product is launched, closing the first sales.

GIST in Business-to-Consumer and Business-to-SMB

When developing and selling products to consumers and small-medium businesses, a lot of things included in this book work in your favor. It's easy to deploy new versions of your software and to measure customer/ user reactions. It's easier (compared to large-business products) to run tests and experiments.

Still, there are common pitfalls to look out for:

- **Skipping idea testing**—When ideas can be developed and deployed in a matter of days or weeks, the question arises: Shouldn't we just launch and see what happens? The answer is that you should strive to test every single idea that is more than a mere low-risk tweak. If you don't, you'll end up with a bloated product that is full of minor features that no one uses. Your code base will bloat too, and pretty soon you'll discover you're no longer able to launch as fast. An easy-to-implement idea may not have to be tested for feasibility, but it should definitely be tested for value, usability, and business viability. You may combine all of those into one A/B test. Doing a full launch with no control group is never the right first step.

- **Not doing qualitative research**—I regularly encounter consumer product teams that never talk directly with customers. Part of the problem is that we are all consumers ourselves, so we feel we understand users well enough to channel them. Nothing is further than the truth. As a product manager for Gmail and YouTube,

I was surprised how much I learned from every conversation I had with a user even though I was a heavy user of both products. As there are many more users, proper segmentation is crucial—you should talk to those users that your idea is targeted at. You should regularly conduct interviews, usability tests, and field research. It's very hard to develop high-impact products without those.

- **Not iterating fast enough**—Even in teams that embrace the principles of agility and lean product development, the rate of processing ideas, churning out steps, and learning is way below what they could and should be doing. This is mostly tied to holding onto old practices of planning and execution, and not fully practicing the concept of investing based on confidence. The rate of testing and learning should be a regular topic of discussion in team retrospectives and management reviews. Measuring and setting targets for those can help accelerate the pace. See Chapter 9 for a list of such metrics.

GIST in Internal Platform/Technology/Services Teams

In many companies, there are product teams developing products or technology to be used by other product teams or by company employees. Some of these include:

- Backend services
- Internal services and apps (for example, room scheduling)
- Reusable software components to be embedded in company products
- Infrastructure for software development, deployment, analytics, security, etc.
- Algorithms and machine-learning models

What's common to these internal teams is that they have a strong engineering base, but often possess just sparse product management, design, and research resources, if any. Sooner or later, it becomes evident that they, too, need those. They have demanding internal users that depend on them. Success is almost invisible to the company, but failure is very clear and often painful. In some cases engineering leads or project managers will fill the gap and assume part-time product management roles.

There is some good news, however. In my experience many platforms and services teams are less tied to traditional plan-and-execute methods (partly because they sustain less pressure from executives and business teams) and are happy to leapfrog directly into evidence-guided approaches like GIST. The other good news is that the customers are right there in the building, ready to be observed, interviewed, and collaborate on designing the products, services, and technology.

The biggest challenges usually revolve around goals, as it's hard for core teams to clearly define what their mission is and how exactly they deliver value and for whom. Should they focus on the company's North Star Metric, or should they make their own? Is success measured by building well-designed systems and technology, in driving usage, or in helping other teams succeed?

Usually, nailing the right model of collaboration with the rest of the organization is key:

- **Service provider model**—In this model, the platform/technology/ services team treats the other employees and teams as their users or customers. This model is best for teams developing internal services, applications, or tools, development infrastructure, and reusable software components. The North Star Metric and submetrics are geared toward value delivered to these internal customers. The benefit of this model is that it enables the team to manage its full GIST stack independently, just like any normal product team.

- **Co-development model**—In this model, members of the team are directly helping other product teams develop and launch products and features. For example, imagine that a team working on a fashion ecommerce service has an idea to allow shoppers to virtually try out shoes using augmented reality on their phones. The team lacks the knowledge to develop the AR part of the feature, so they reach out to the internal machine-vision team for help. In this case, setting up a customer/contractor relationship between the two teams will be cumbersome and hamper agility and speed. A better model is to create a virtual team with members from both teams that share a set of goals having to do with the shoppers themselves. The virtual team can own its GIST planning and execution stack, and iteratively develop the idea and test it. The machine-vision team measures itself on its contribution to the North Star Metric of the company, and thus can choose to partake in ideas that have the highest potential. This model works well also for backend teams where members can semi-permanently attach to various product teams, thus making "backend" an integral part of every team rather than a service provider.

GIST in Multi-sided Marketplaces/Services

Companies developing multi-sided marketplaces or multi-sided services have to cater to two or more types of users/customers: buyers and sellers, drivers and passengers, publishers and advertisers, and so on. The common approach is to have different product teams, or product groups, work to deliver and capture value to each type of customer. Still, the success of a service stems first and foremost from its ability to connect supply with demand and to foster value exchange between the users themselves. Therefore, there's typically a third type of team that focuses on the success of the marketplace or platform itself in connecting supply with demand.

All of these teams and groups develop together one complex product, which isn't easy, especially considering there is usually also a big operational side to running the service/platform. Let's see how the GIST model can help.

Goals, Metrics, Ideas

North Star Metric—The ideal NSM is one that measures the total value being exchanged through the marketplace or platform. In Chapter 2, we saw two examples: eBay's NSM is gross merchandise volume (GMV), Airbnb uses Nights Booked. For a ride-hailing service a reasonable NSM would be Monthly Trips Completed; for a job site, number of positions filled. You want to measure as close as possible to the value experience. If buyers and sellers transact inside your platform, then your job is easy. However, that's not the case for many multi-sided services. You therefore have to find indications that value is about to be exchanged (for example multiple messages exchanged, including what looks like a phone number or email) or was exchanged (for example a listing removed with reason "Sold").

Submetrics—Contributing to the NSM will be a user-specific metric, such as success rate in onboarding a new property owner, as well as metrics that measure how well supply matches demand (aka liquidity), how efficient the platform is at helping each side find the other, and the rate at which value is successfully exchanged. Different teams may own different metrics, but there's always going to be some overlap and cross-effects.

OKRs—As usual, we want each team to be able to work independently on its goals, for example helping drivers grow their income, ensuring passengers feel safe and secure, and reducing the number of passengers without a ride in the late-afternoon rush hour. Many goals span the team boundaries. Improving Search is both a platform goal and a demand-side goal. Shared OKRs as well as building virtual teams can help in setting such goals.

Ideas and steps—Despite how intimately intertwined the work may be, you want to create an environment where teams can pursue their ideas and steps without tight central coordination. Following Netflix's principle *Strategically aligned, but loosely coupled,* means creating good company-level or business-unit level goals and then allowing the teams to operate with loose coordination. Broadly sharing GIST boards will help with communication. Product managers and middle managers also play an important role in coordinating the efforts of different parts of the platform and avoiding nasty surprises. Sometimes it makes sense to build a cross-team virtual team to work on a specific goal.

Many steps will require testing on two or more sides of the marketplace/service at once, but they don't all have to use the same validation techniques. For example you may run a beta test for a new idea featuring a near-complete user interface for the buyer side, while on the seller side use a concierge test using emails and phone calls to collect and enter necessary information. After you've validated the assumptions on the buyer side you can further develop and test the seller side.

GIST in Physical Products

Intuitively, we may assume physical products are exempt from much of the evidence-guided playbook. As development cycles are typically longer and more costly, and shipping the wrong product is very hard to fix, the tendency is to stay with detailed, deliberate planning followed by exact execution. Product discovery is great for software products, the thinking goes, but not for physical products.

But of course this is not true.

To begin with, the difference between hardware and software is rapidly thinning. If you're developing a hardware product, chances are you're developing a software product that runs on non-standard hardware (but is likely not completely custom-made, either). The customer will need to get both, but you can develop them almost independently and with different cycles—the software is likely to change at a much higher rate and can in many cases be upgraded after the product is in the hands of customers. This means that the product keeps evolving and improving. Smartphones demonstrated this model, and now many physical products follow. Tesla demonstrated this to great effect when it pushed a firmware update that increased the top speed and range of its Model 3 cars practically overnight.[4]

If your product is connected to the Internet, you stand to gain many of the benefits of an app or a web service, including continuous deployments, real-time usage data and error reports—even A/B experiments.

But perhaps your physical product cannot easily tap into the benefit of software and the Internet. Does that mean there are no opportunities to create learning loops prior to the launch? Consider these examples as inspiration:

- In 1995, Team New Zealand surprised everyone by defeating the, until then, unbeatable American team in the prestigious America's Cup yacht race. In *The Principles of Product Development Flow*, Donald G. Reinertsen explains how they designed a superior yacht that helped secure this win: "*When they tested improvements in keel designs, they used two virtually identical boats. The unimproved boat would sail against the improved boat to determine the effect of a design change. By sailing one boat against the other, they were able to discriminate against small changes in performance very quickly.*"

In contrast, the competing American design team used a single boat supplemented by computer models and NASA wind tunnels."[5]

- Fashion company Inditex, best known for its brand Zara, tags every item of clothing with an RFID microchip that enables it to be tracked until it is sold to customers. Sales and inventory data are sent in real time back to Inditex's data center. Every morning Zara's design team goes over the previous day's sales data, as well as qualitative feedback from sales employees ("customers don't like the zipper"). Combining fashion sense and analytics they determine trends, define hypotheses such as "yellow dresses with pockets are in demand," and create designs accordingly. The new designs are first ordered from manufacturers in small batches and arrive in test stores within two to three weeks. Designs that sell well are produced in larger volumes, while those that don't sell are discontinued. Overall, 50 percent of items are designed and manufactured in the middle of a season based on what becomes popular.[6]

But is it really possible to test early with incomplete physical products? You bet. There are many and varied ways to prototype and test physical products:

- Enclosures and interfaces can be first modeled using paper, cardboard, wood, clay, even Lego bricks, and then made more realistic using 3D printing, CNC, and other methods.

- Electronics prototypes consisting of breadboards and off-the-shelf electronics can be used to create functioning appliances without requiring custom-printed circuit boards. FPGA (field programmable gate arrays) and ASIC (application-specific integrated circuit) can be used long before we're ready to manufacture custom chips en masse.

- Computerized prototypes can be implemented using single-board computers such as Raspberry Pi and Arduino, mobile phones and tablets, mini-PCs, and any other small computer you have lying around.

When all else fails, you can take an existing product and rebrand it. This is what General Electric did when it created a six-month project to test the assumptions behind a new type of diesel engine that normally would take five years to develop. Eric Ries, who advised GE, tells the story in his book *The Startup Way*.[7] The company realized that it could take one of its existing engines, codenamed "616," modify it to produce the power required, and test it in the most important scenario that the yet-to-be-built engine was designed to serve. The team was able not only to test and learn, but also to sell a few of these minimum-viable-products that were fully functional, although less profitable. The GE product manager, Cory Nelson, recounts that the MVP was also important because it gave the managers of the project something concrete (i.e., evidence) to show to company management early on.[8]

The Missing Piece

I hope I have convinced you that evidence-guided development can be used in your company. GIST, specifically, is an adaptable model, and one that can work in a broad set of circumstances. Still, even if the framework is right for your organization, a big question looms: Would your managers and coworkers be willing to accept it and adapt the way they work? In the next chapter, we'll see how to drive the change and successfully introduce GIST into your own organization.

Takeaways

- To benefit from evidence-guided development, enterprise B2B companies need to operate as *product companies*, building packaged products that can be sold over and over, and create *product teams*, rather than *feature teams* or *delivery teams*.

- Customer requests can be evaluated using ICE, factoring in potential gains in the top metrics if the feature is implemented, and losses if it is not. Behind these requests there's usually a more complicated story and often there's more than one way to tackle them.

- Contrary to common thinking, B2B product teams can test assumptions and product ideas. They have a variety of validation techniques available including interviews, early adopter programs, data analysis and concierge tests, and pilots. It's best not to start selling the product during the discovery phase.

- GIST is easier for B2C companies to adopt, but some fall into common traps of skipping testing for cheap ideas, not conducting qualitative research, and testing too slowly.

- Internal platforms and services teams are often in a better position to adopt evidence-guided approaches as they face fewer demands from managers and the business, and at the same time have their customers in-house to observe and test with.

- Internal platform and services teams that work as service providers should focus goals and metrics on their internal customers, rather than the company's customers. If they work in a co-development model they can aim to contribute to the goals of the company.

- Multi-sided marketplaces/platforms usually have dedicated product teams for each side of the service, and other teams to make sure the service connects supply with demand well. Each of these teams can create its own goals, ideas, steps, and tasks, but they are much more closely intertwined.

- In a multi-sided marketplace/platform many ideas will span two or more sides of the service; however, those can be tested with different validation techniques, allowing one side of the idea to be developed and validated first.

- Evidence-guided development can be used with physical products as well, despite there being more limitations. Many hardware devices have a software component that can be developed, tested, and updated with faster cycles. Enclosures, logic boards, and integrated devices can also be tested and iterated on. Even fashion items and racing yachts can be rapidly designed and improved on using an evidence-guided approach.

Notes

[1] "The Slippery Slope of Sales-Led Development – Rich Mironov." Nov. 2, 2018, https://www.mironov.com/sales-led/. Accessed Jul. 30, 2020.

[2] "Product vs. Feature Teams | Silicon Valley Product Group" Aug. 29, 2019, https://svpg.com/product-vs-feature-teams/. Accessed Jul. 30, 2020.

[3] "The Sales Learning Curve – Harvard Business Review." https://hbr.org/2006/07/the-sales-learning-curve. Accessed Jul. 3, 2020.

[4] "Tesla remotely increases power output of all Model 3 vehicles through software update", Mar. 18 2019, https://electrek.co/2019/03/18/tesla-remotely-increases-power-output-of-all-model-3-vehicles-through-software-update/

[5] Reinertsen, Donald G. 2009. *The Principles of Product Development Flow*, Celeritas Pub, https://www.amazon.com/Principles-Product-Development-Flow-Generation/dp/1935401009

[6] "ZARA: Achieving the 'Fast' in Fast Fashion through Analytics." Apr. 5, 2017, https://digital.hbs.edu/platform-digit/submission/zara-achieving-the-fast-in-fast-fashion-through-analytics/. Accessed Jul. 28, 2020.

[7] Ries, Eric. 2017. *The Startup Way: How Modern Companies Use Entrepreneurial Management to Transform Culture & Drive Long-Term Growth*, Currency, http://www.thestartupway.com/

[8] "Cory Nelson, The Diesel Engine MVP, LSC14 – YouTube." Dec. 19, 2014, https://www.youtube.com/watch?v=b1ReChbK1r4. Accessed Jul. 28, 2020.

CHAPTER 9

Adopting GIST

Switching to an evidence-guided mode of work is rarely easy. The people developing the product and influencing it have to change the way they work and think, often in counterintuitive ways. Your managers, stakeholders, and team members may resist the change, and for good reasons. They are entrusted with important responsibilities and they have things to protect—revenue, budgets, customer relationships, product quality... People's reputations and careers are also on the line.

In my experience most people will be supportive of a model like GIST once they undergo training, and they understand what the change entails, and how it is going to help the company and their area of responsibility. Still there's a big difference between supporting a big change in principle and actually going through with it. You should expect to run into adoption hurdles and objections. In the first part of this chapter we'll go over the most common challenges, including mistrust, lack of time, and lack of resources, and discuss ideas how to overcome them.

Even when everyone is onboard, the transition may run slow and be hard to complete. Some organizations take a very long time to implement GIST, and lose momentum midway. Others try to do too much too fast and get overwhelmed and fatigued. Yet others pick and choose, eventually creating just a slightly more sophisticated version of the old system. Personnel changes and reorgs bring new managers and employees into the fold and can cause regressions and setbacks.

The second part of this chapter covers change patterns that will smooth out the transition and give you a better chance of success. To make things more concrete I'll talk specifically about adopting the GIST model, but the guidelines and principles apply broadly to other changes you might strive to drive.

Common Adoption Challenges

Lack of Trust

When I teach GIST to managers and executives, I often hear that they'd love to use it, but the product teams are too inexperienced, or lack the "right culture" to take on this sort of responsibility. Team members are just as enthusiastic, but quick to point out that management is sales-driven, top-down, and waterfall-ish, hence incapable of adopting the mindset GIST requires. Both groups will only half-commit to the change as they don't trust the other group to do its part.

Mistrust is a very serious problem. It often stems from self-reinforcing beliefs about others, amplified by cycles of failure. As companies grow and introduce middle management, departmental silos, and processes, it becomes that much easier to lose trust in colleagues and managers.

We can't wave a magic wand and make people trust each other. Trust has to be earned and learned. The trick is to carve a safe area to allow people to show what they're capable of. It may be one pilot project, or one team, but it's better to test across a number of teams and projects, just in case we fall on the wrong side of the statistics. It's also best to plan for this test to run at least a full quarter, though two is better.

As we go through with the first implementation it's important to enforce these guidelines:

- Extreme transparency—The managers should be very open about their priorities and rationale, and share a lot of context. Product teams should be very transparent about the ideas and steps they're choosing and their reasonings. Regularly reviewing the GIST board we saw in Chapter 5 can be very helpful.

- Evidence rather than opinions—Jim Barksdale, the former CEO of Netscape, is famous for saying: "If we have data, let's look at data. If all we have are opinions, let's go with mine." That's great advice. If you want a manager to trust what you're suggesting you'd better arm yourself with evidence. The more you demonstrate you do your homework the more your manager will be inclined to trust your judgment.

- Play by the rules—The agreement should be that everyone involved, including managers and stakeholders, will play by the new rules for the entire period. There should be an objective arbiter (similar to a scrummaster in Scrum), typically a VP or director of product or an external coach. This person will call out infringements.

From experience, people are pleasantly surprised to be proven wrong about one another. I've seen employees whose head was on the chopping block for "lacking initiative" turn into star performers. I witnessed over-controlling managers become staunch supporters of idea banks and ICE scores. It may take awhile, but we eventually replace the vicious cycle of mistrust with a virtuous cycle of transparency, evidence, and built-up trust.

Missing Resources

Some companies wait, sometimes indefinitely, for an analytics system, a test infrastructure, or a team of user researchers and data analysts to be put in place before starting to use the new model. These are all important things and should be high on the priority list of any organization (by the way, this is one of the few exceptions to the "no output goals" rule.) Unfortunately, often they are not, which means the change may never happen.

You don't need Google-level infrastructure to validate ideas. Referring back to the AFTER model we saw in Chapter 4, most of the Assessment and Fact-Finding validation techniques are things any product team can do. Anyone can assess ideas on paper using ICE, assumption mapping, and stakeholder reviews. Anyone can interview customers and conduct usability tests. It's a great bonus if you have a user researcher to help, but you can learn to do them yourself (there are many good books and courses to teach you how), or hire a contractor or a research service. Digging through data without an analytics system or a data analyst is possible with help from backend engineers, or better, by learning how to query the database on your own. Charting can be done in Excel or Google Docs. Most forms of early tests—fake doors, concierge, Wizard of Oz—don't require any special infrastructure. Dogfood, early adopter tests, betas are something most product teams can do with their existing resources. A/B testing does require infrastructure, know-how, and sufficient amounts of data, but in many cases you can make do with other types of testing until these are in place.

No Time

Your managers and colleagues may be in favor of adopting GIST, but have a plausible reason why *now* is not the right time:

- We're in the midst of an important planning process
- We have to finish an important project
- We have a list of must-have features to complete

Much like the woodsman who is working hard and slow cutting down trees with a blunt ax because he doesn't have time to sharpen his ax, because he has too many trees to cut, it's hard for us to stop our train of work in favor of making this work more efficient and productive. In reality, there'll never be a perfect time to start the transition. New planning sessions and must-have projects are just around the corner. Besides, GIST is very likely to make your plans and top features moot. Starting to plan and execute in terms of goals, ideas, steps, and tasks as soon as possible is likely to save you much time and effort. Much like getting in shape or quitting smoking, *now* is the right time to start, and the more you delay the less likely you are to do it.

We don't necessarily have to stop everything and make a clear break, though. As we'll see, a *gradual* adoption is often more effective. So there will be room for some of the work-in-progress to proceed. Still, in the areas we do wish to change the agreement should be that we start right away, and make it a high priority.

Attachment to Roadmaps

Some people in your company, especially in Sales and Marketing, may object to taking away time-based release roadmaps for one or more of these reasons:

- They wish to promote and sell the new features/products in advance
- They wish to plan their work throughout the year

- They perceive the roadmap as a type of contract that holds the product teams accountable (yet another form of mistrust)
- The roadmap creates a (false) sense of security

Trying to convince business folk of the merits of lean/agile philosophies is rarely sufficient. A better approach is to discuss how well roadmaps are serving the business today. It's usually not hard to show that last year's roadmap didn't materialize quite as envisioned and certainly didn't create the expected business results. Trying to do more of the same is likely to just produce more bad results.

What you may discover is that many of your colleagues are not necessarily in love with roadmaps, but they consider them necessary as they don't know there are alternatives. You may suggest replacing output roadmaps with *Outcome Roadmaps* (see Chapter 6 for an example)—a visual way to show the commitment of the product teams to business goals. Note that outcome roadmaps can also include some high-confidence ideas that were already validated, so they partially overlap with output roadmaps. The roadmap decision should stem from a discussion on the *real* needs of the organization, and how we may best address them.

Fear of Losing Control of the Product

Adopting GIST may mean that managers and stakeholders will have to relinquish some of their godlike powers to decide which product ideas are better than others. They may naturally be reluctant to do this as they need to protect and grow the business.

Here it's important to first explain, and then demonstrate, that it's not about turning managers and stakeholders into silent observers while the product teams do all the driving. On the contrary, the system will only work if these folks are heavily involved and influencing. We are substituting one form of control—choosing ideas—with another—choosing goals. What is lost in direct control over product deliverables is gained in control over the outcomes that the teams are trying to produce. It's leadership instead of management.

Once we manage to create the first true GIST cycles, and managers and stakeholders see how things work (transparency is key here), the discussion becomes much easier. Still, beware of innovative ways to "improve" the process that are actually wrangling power back ("The opinion of the CMO should be considered market data" or "The sales team is responsible for setting impact and confidence in the ICE scores").

Fear of Slowing Down

Some managers and engineers may worry that GIST will reduce "implementation velocity." Another variant is the concern that the engineering team will not be 100 percent utilized.

An important first step is to agree what's better—full-throttle development of the wrong thing, or slower and more cautious iteration toward the right thing? The question is actually about whether we want to aim for output (code) or outcomes (value). GIST isn't trying to shorten time-to-market, but time-to-value, which is the time to achieve an outcome.

Second, as we've seen in Chapter 4, GIST projects are both faster and more resource-efficient than classic plan-and-execute projects. There are multiple reasons why this is the case, but the most important is that we limit the effort invested in bad ideas (which may amount to up to 90 percent of all ideas). If you're handy with spreadsheets, it's possible to whip up a rough calculation of the savings in time and effort GIST will bring. Here are a couple of articles for inspiration: a) In a thought experiment[1] I calculated that a team using evidence-guided methods can 10x its outcomes while reducing output, and b) B2B product management expert Rich Mironov calculates[2] the massive waste companies can save by adopting product discovery.

An important step forward would be to weed out any goals—explicit or implicit—that are about launch dates, velocity, scope, utilization, story points, or any other form of output. It's hard to get people to optimize for outcomes when they're being measured on output.

The concern that the team will sit idle is rarely warranted. If there's not enough product work temporarily, the team can work on those important engineering, design, or infrastructure ideas that always seem to be pushed back. Even better, they can help product managers, designers, and researchers conduct research. Lastly, there's no real imperative to keep the team working at full capacity all the time. Sporadic downtime is actually a good buffer for the overtime the team faces when it's under pressure to launch.

Fear of Over-Analysis

Some managers worry that an evidence-guided system like GIST can get the company stuck in "analysis paralysis." Second-guessing ourselves and testing repeatedly seems slow and indecisive to them. In their view, going all-in is the way to build products.

This is not an invalid concern; it's certainly possible to overdo idea prioritization and experimentation. If you find that you're spending hours each week on ICE-scoring ideas, or taking six steps to validate a one-week feature, you're probably doing it wrong.

Still, companies are far more likely to waste time in roadmap and product debates than in idea analysis. Lengthy projects are much more likely to cause deliberation over requirements, design, project plans, and launch plans than steps and learning milestones would. A GIST project is a very dynamic thing. ICE analysis cuts through lengthy idea debates and steps drive toward action. Most of the time is spent on developing versions of the idea and conducting tests, not on analysis and discussion.

Not Right for Our Type of Product or Business

I must have heard by now every variant of "Good idea, but not for us." Some managers and employees feel that GIST or the principles underlying it are simply not applicable to their special case. Reasons may include offering a high-touch enterprise-grade product, developing products that are subject to regulation, creating physical products, and more, but underlying those is usually a belief that in your particular case either there's no uncertainty—you just know what needs to be built—or there's no way to truly test ideas except for building and launching.

In Chapters 7 and 8 we saw a variety of company archetypes and how they can use GIST. Still, it's possible that your business or product is fundamentally different. The relevant questions to ask are:

- Can and should we define goals in terms of outcomes?
- Can there be more than one way to achieve the goals?
- Is it possible that our product ideas will not pan out as expected (or even fail)?
- Is there anything we can do to better evaluate these ideas before, during, and after we build them?

- Should we involve the product teams in goal definition, idea prioritization, and step planning?

I struggle to think of an organization where the answer to all or even most of these questions is *no*. On close inspection, the seemingly non-negotiable principles that prevent us from changing the way we work turn out to be less real than we think (usually, it takes a more agile competitor to prove this to us). The annals of history are full of good companies that didn't challenge their assumptions or were not able to alter their playbooks.

Perfectionism

Testing our ideas early and often means putting incomplete and unpolished versions of our products in front of real users and customers. Some of your colleagues may understandably worry about confusing or annoying users, destroying their trust in the product, or hurting the brand. For others, compromising on product scope, user experience, or code quality is a major no-no. Education and experience tell them to never cut corners.

When confronted with this type of objection, it's important to make clear that: a) We will not compromise on quality or completeness of the final product; b) Only a small subset of users or customers will be exposed to the interim versions; c) Given the option, most users would take a limited and rough product that does exactly what they need, over a feature-rich, well-polished product that delivers little value. Think of early Google Docs vs. Microsoft Office, or most early mobile apps compared to their desktop counterparts.

In practice, this type of objection tends to fade away as it becomes apparent that a very partial version of the right product can generate strong, positive user/customer response.

We're Already Doing It

This is an objection I hear a lot from middle managers: "We already have something like GIST in place." It's perfectly possible that you have things under control; however, it usually takes a short discussion with other employees and managers to discover a more nuanced reality. Sure, there are processes in place for goal-setting, idea prioritization, and carrying out experiments, but are they working as expected? Do they create the desired effects?

The following scorecard will help you measure how close you are to applying the spirit of GIST as presented in this book.

GIST Scorecard

For each item below enter a score of 0%–100% showing how much you're practicing this element of the system. Then you can average the scores in each category—goals, ideas, steps, tasks—and average again across categories to get your final score.

- **Goals**
    - We identified what impact (value delivered and value captured) means for us and are measuring impact using a very small set of top-level metrics ____%
    - We mapped out multiple levels of submetrics that contribute to our top metrics, and know how they are interconnected ____%
    - All goals are expressed in terms of outcomes (measurable improvements) and not output (things we will do) ____%
    - All teams have team-level goals which they define ____%
    - Goals are well aligned top-down, bottom-up, and across ____%

    Goals average score ____%

- **Ideas**
    - We're constantly collecting ideas and are willing to evaluate any idea no matter where it comes from ____%
    - Each team manages its own list of ideas that is open for anyone to see ____%
    - We pick ideas on the basis of their impact, ease, and supporting evidence (confidence) ____%

    Ideas average score ____%

- **Steps**
  - All ideas are validated through at least one form of test, experiment, or release test before fully launching ____%
  - We re-evaluate ideas based on test results ____%
  - Ideas that don't produce supporting evidence are modified or parked ____%

  Steps average ____%

- **Tasks**
  - Team members are involved in defining goals, ideas, and validation steps ____%
  - All teams regularly and frequently review the status of goals, ideas, and steps and update them as necessary ____%
  - All tasks (sprint items or Kanban cards) are clearly associated with one or more discovery or delivery steps ____%

  Tasks average score ____%

  Total score: ____% [average across Goals, Ideas, Steps, and Tasks]

We're Already Using Another Methodology

Some organizations attempt to find a compromise between GIST and another methodology they've already adopted, trying to satisfy supporters of both approaches. This can work when there's lots of common ground in philosophy and implementation. For example, GIST is very compatible with true agile development, design thinking, and growth hacking. (In fact, the champions of these approaches within companies often tell me that GIST is helping them do their jobs.) At other times, the merger leads to a confusing compromise that is of little value to the organization. Marrying incompatible processes doesn't work. It's better to choose one or the other.

Driving the Change

Change is hard, especially one that touches so many aspects of the product and business. Here are practices I've observed in companies that were most successful in adopting and changing the way they work.

Make the Case for the Change

In most organizations, this sort of change requires a decision by top executives. You shouldn't come to this discussion only armed with self-conviction. It's best to make your case backed by facts and evidence.

Here are a few things to focus on:

- The shortfalls of the current planning-and-execution process and how much it is costing us today (tread carefully here not to put anyone on the spot).

- The benefits the company should see from the new process: true agility, customer focus, evidence-based decision-making, increased team empowerment, decreased management overhead, and shorter planning cycles. How will these translate into better business results, higher customer satisfaction and cost savings?

- The Confidence Meter. I was surprised to find that the Confidence Meter is the thing that many management teams get most excited about. It makes sense—the C-level team is flooded with funding requests backed by little more than opinions and salesmanship. The Confidence Meter and ICE scores give them the tools to both evaluate such requests objectively and to guide reports to focus on evidence rather than hype.

The bottom line: a) We're wasting a massive part of our resources today producing the wrong things, b) By not adopting evidence-guided thinking we're exposing ourselves to a risk that more nimble and adaptive competitors will move in on our business.

Find an Executive Sponsor

Another common success pattern is having an executive, usually C-level, take responsibility for the success of GIST. This person will act as GIST champion inside the C-suite, working with other executives to explain, convince, and set a plan of action. The sponsor will make sure to train everyone who needs to know about GIST. Then, during the implementation phase, she'll make time in her busy schedule to attend implementation sessions personally and coax people to do things right. The champion is there to remind everyone that the company is taking this matter seriously in events or internal communication as well as in goals and incentives.

Teach the Methodology Broadly

Your chances of successfully launching GIST in your org grow significantly if everyone understands exactly what it entails. North Star Metric, OKRs, idea banks, and validation steps may be common terms in the industry, but interpretations can vary widely. The operation of GIST as a system may seem simple at a glance, but entails many nuances in practice. Beyond the surface-level processes you want to teach the underlying models and principles. If all these are not well understood, you might face misalignment, friction, and pushback.

For these reasons, I suggest teaching GIST broadly in the organization. This can be accomplished through training and/or by reading this book. At a minimum, you'll want to train product managers, designers, engineering leads, and the managers of these folks, as well as key stakeholders that can serve as ambassadors for GIST in their own organizations. I also recommend running condensed GIST workshops for executives (director level up to C-suite) and for cross-functional product teams (rank-and-file engineers and designers).

The goal of the training round is to have a shared understanding of:

- The principles
- The terms
- The methodology
- Who owns what

Gradual Rollout—Start Where the Pain Is

Some companies are in a rush to implement GIST all at once. I often recommend against this. Too many things will need to change in parallel and the ramp-up curve may be too steep. If you have a big gap to close, I suggest staging the adoption. GIST is a modular system—you can implement certain layers first and others later. So start by looking at the four layers of GIST and consider where the biggest challenges in the company lie today.

- In companies where the direction is unclear or constantly changing, where there are big challenges in alignment, or where focus on users and customers is low, I recommend starting by implementing the Goals layer of GIST: the North Star Metric, outcome roadmaps, and outcomes-based objectives and key results.

- In organizations that spend lots of time debating ideas, where ideas are chosen based on opinions, consensus, or weak evidence, and where there's a track record of investment in bad ideas, I recommend introducing the Idea layer first—idea banks and ICE scores, often coupled with beefing up user/market/tech research.

- In companies where projects are long and expensive, where little or no testing and learning takes place during the project, and where results are generally disappointing, I suggest adopting the Steps layer first. Build learning milestones and customer feedback loops into projects, utilize the AFTER model, analyze results objectively, and be bold about pivoting or even stopping projects that don't work.

- If, in your organization, development teams seem submerged in their own world and disconnected from the needs of users and the business, engineering and design projects take an inordinate amount of time, or you have to create mountains of specifications and user stories, I would suggest using some of the techniques we saw in Chapter 5, especially the GIST board or a similar project tracking tool that gives the team a broader view and makes it an active contributor. This will entail introducing some experimentation (steps) too.

Obviously, the four layers of GIST are all connected, but to get started, a North Star Metric is the only bit of plumbing you must have (and is therefore the first thing to figure out). The NSM will enable you to rank ideas, evaluate steps, and build early GIST boards where sometimes the only goal is to grow the NSM.

Set Ambitious-yet-Realistic Goals

No one can turn into a marathon runner overnight or shed 30 pounds within a week. Success comes from setting ambitious-yet-realistic targets and sticking to them. The same is true for your adoption of evidence-guided thinking. During the transition period you'll need to work on two types of outcomes at the same time:

- Business/user outcomes (like the ones we saw in Chapter 2)

- Self-improvement outcomes that describe the change you want to create at the end of every quarter and year

What are these outcomes? We can get an idea by looking at the core operation of GIST:

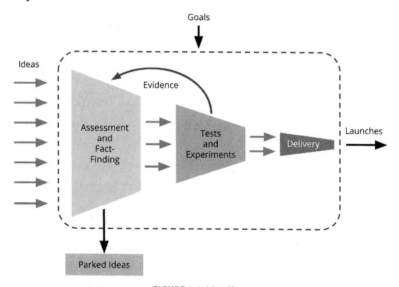

FIGURE 9.1: Idea Flow

Based on this picture, these metrics can help you calibrate your progress:

- The total number of ideas evaluated per quarter (using, at minimum, ICE analysis and goals alignment)

- Number of ideas tested per quarter

- The number of ideas released per quarter

- Total number of tests and experiments conducted per month
- Percent of steps that generated learning (i.e., where we were able to rescore the idea and/or generate useful insights based on the evidence collected)
- Percent of ideas launched at least with a medium Confidence level (per the Confidence Meter)
- Percent of ideas released that generate measurable outcome improvements

The first four metrics are aligned with Linus Pauling's observation that the way to have good ideas is to test many ideas. However, these are outputs, and may be meaningless unless we're able to learn and create outcomes, which is what the latter three metrics measure. These seven core metrics should give you the main outcomes to work toward. If you're only testing three ideas per quarter, push yourself to test ten in the next one. If only 10% of ideas hit medium confidence prior to launch, try to reach 20%, then 30%, and keep improving.

Other things you may wish to measure:
- The ratio of outcomes-based goals out of all goals
- The ratio of teams that develop their own goals
- Ratio of employees reporting that they are working toward clear outcomes, and have the necessary context to understand why these outcomes are important
- The ratio of ideas that stem from outside research rather than inside ideation

And all of these metrics should ideally go down:
- Time spent on planning
- Number of sales escalation or management mandates per quarter
- The number of output-based incentives
- % ideas slowed down due to dependencies or processes
- Average time to launch an idea

You may wonder what you should aim for. There's no fixed number I can give you, and the goal should be to continuously improve (more on this later) rather than to hit a certain fixed goal and stop. Still, if after six months of using GIST, you only manage to evaluate on average five ideas per month, and test one, you probably have some way to go before you start seeing the benefits.

I would start measuring the key metrics right now, before you've implemented GIST, so you'll have a baseline to compare against. The current numbers may be depressingly low, but this is normal. Use this fact as evidence in your discussions with management and stakeholders for why you should adopt GIST.

Making Incremental Improvements

Many big changes come from a series of incremental improvements rather than one big leap. In Chapter 7 I told you how between 2008 and 2011 Hewlett Packard's LaserJet Firmware division, consisting of 400 employees across multiple offices, had managed to rewrite its platform, introduce automated testing, and launch continuous integrations through a series of four-week iterations each with its own target set of outcomes (for example "P1 issues open < 1 week"). The book *Toyota Kata*[3] recounts a similar pattern of continuous self-improvement that stands at the heart of the famous Toyota Production System (TPS)—the principle known as *Kaizen*.

The incremental improvement approach can work for adoption of GIST as well. Instead of waiting for the end of the quarter to measure progress, the product organization can set quicker cycles of self-improvement in which it tries to boost idea evaluation, experimentation, team autonomy, or anything else we identified as a key goal. The shorter cycles make the change concrete and less intimidating. Instead of trying to climb the entire mountain, we choose a much lower target we can potentially achieve by next month. Just the act of trying (and often failing) provides real evidence, helps surface core issues, and motivates good discussions. Over time self-improvement becomes a habit of the product organization or even the entire company. With continuous iteration and learning, success is bound to arrive, first slowly, but then at an accelerated rate. When it does it should be shared and celebrated broadly.

Build an Operative Team

While the sponsor is pushing GIST forward, you'll need people on the ground to steer day-to-day adoption. It's a good idea to assemble a small GIST task force composed of a few senior and respected product managers, designers, engineers, researchers, and business stakeholders who are genuinely excited about driving the change. This team can take different names—task force, coaches, steering group, council, guild—and operate in different ways. The team should meet regularly to set goals, assess progress (see the scorecard and metrics in Chapter 6), and deal with setbacks and challenges. Its main job, though, is to persistently motivate and assist teams as they implement GIST.

Meet the Protagonist of this Story

Ultimately, many changes start from within. If you like GIST, it may be up to *you* to take the lead in driving this change in your organization, or at minimum, to be the spark that ignites a flame. How to do it depends on your personal style and on your company makeup and culture.

Find like-minded coworkers and colleagues who feel the way you do about improving your organization and who are willing to work with you to support implementing GIST. Talk patiently yet persistently, one-on-one with key managers and stakeholders. Recruit the executive sponsor. Pitch to top management. Create an operative team. Follow up with product teams. It's hard work, but ultimately your managers, and coworkers, will thank you for driving the change and will recognize your contribution to the success of the company. My hope is that now that you've read this book, you're fully armed and excited to do it.

Takeaways

- Change is hard, especially when it's going against company beliefs and norms. In this chapter we reviewed 11 common types of challenges you may encounter, and ways to counter them.

- Lack of trust is a severe problem that is likely hurting you already today. In my experience transparency, discussing evidence, and clear rules of operation can help product teams gradually earn trust from managers and stakeholders.

- Attachment to release roadmaps and fear that development velocity will slide down are preventing some companies from adopting evidence-guided development. The approach I suggest is to show that both roadmaps and output-focus are creating massive waste (which can be estimated in actual dollar or euro numbers).

- Some pushback stems from the belief that evidence-guided thinking isn't right for your type of company or market, or that it is about launching sloppy products to the market. Both are misconceptions that I hope that information contained in this book can dispel.

- Some leaders are convinced they are already working in an evidence-guided mode. I included a scorecard to help you test where you really stand.

- Before starting to implement it's good to get buy-in by making the case—the shortfalls of the current system and the potential gains from the new—and by teaching the new methods broadly.

- Aim for *gradual* adoption rather than a big-bang. For a company who has quite a big gap (see the scorecard) expect multiple quarters, and often up to a year of rollout. Start with the layer where currently the biggest pain lives: Goals, Ideas. Steps, or Tasks.

- This chapter lists a number of metrics you can track and set goals for that are based on the funnels of discovery and delivery (for example the % of ideas tested that generated learning.) It's best not to wait a whole three months to try and improve on those, but rather work in shorter, self-improvement (Kaizen) cycles with smaller goals.

- It's important to have at least one executive sponsor who will make adoption of evidence-guided thinking a priority with the executive teams, and will create the space and allocate the resources needed for adoption. On the ground there should be a steering group that will facilitate and support the change, measure progress, and report back to management.

Notes

[1] Gilad, Itamar. "Stop Obsessing Over Development Velocity, Focus on This Instead." *Itamar Gilad*, Feb. 11, 2021, https://itamargilad.com/velocity-vs-impact/

[2] Mironov, Rich. "Product Waste and The ROI of Discovery." *Rich Mironov*, May 24, 2022, https://www.mironov.com/waste/. Accessed Apr. 27, 2023.

[3] Rother, Mike. 2009. *Toyota Kata: Managing People for Improvement, Adaptiveness and Superior Results*, McGraw Hill Professional.

Endnote
(and How You Can Help)

Four and a half years ago I sat down to write this book optimistically hoping to be done in 12 months. What followed was a series of classical blunders, many of which I warn against in this book. There was output-focus, unrealistic timelines, fuzzy goals, scope-creep, perfectionism, and general procrastination. I spent 14 months producing a manuscript that no one liked, and then another three years pivoting and rewriting it. Luckily I had some evidence to guide me. The feedback I got from beta readers and from industry experts helped me iterate, cut out a lot of unnecessary staff and focus the book on what matters.

I won't lie, this was the hardest project I have ever worked on. What kept me going was my own notion of impact. I imagined product people reading this book, finding answers to problems that trouble them, and maybe changing the way they work. I wished to make evidence-guided development a more concrete and actionable thing, one that more companies can practice. I hoped to make a small but meaningful dent in the high walls protecting opinion-based development.

You can help me amplify the message. People (and book site algorithms) often judge books based on reader reviews and ratings. Leaving a review on Amazon or on your favorite book site will go a long way in helping people discover this book. I would very much appreciate it, and I'm sure other people will too.

Thanks for reading.

Itamar

What's Next?

There's obviously a lot more to evidence-guided development. You may have questions and you're sure to need more information during your journey. Here are some resources to help.

The companion page of this book EvidenceGuided.com/BookResources offers supplementary reading and resources that are constantly kept up to date. Here's what you'll find:

- Downloadable tools and templates—the Confidence Meter spreadsheet, GIST board, and more
- Related articles, eBooks, and books
- Clarifications and FAQs about the content of this book
- Lists of metrics, tools, and other resources you might find helpful

All the content on the page is free of charge, but you may have to subscribe to my newsletter for some of the downloads.

Courses—It's one thing reading about product approaches and techniques, and another practicing them hands-on and critiquing the results. For this reason I offer courses (live and self-paced) to help build up your knowledge and skills. I have workshops designed for product leads, for team members, and for executives. Check out: EvidenceGuided.com/courses

Keynotes—If you need help inspiring and informing your colleagues and managers, I'd be happy to share some of my experiences and learnings based on over 25 years of product development. See: itamargilad.com/keynotes

Consulting—If you want to talk and get my advice visit: itamargilad.com/consulting

My Newsletter—In my monthly newsletter *High-Impact Product Management* I share articles, news, and new tools. Sign up here: itamargilad.com/newsletter

Acknowledgments

This book would not have been possible without the help and support of many kind and insightful people.

I'd like to thank the adopters of the GIST model over the years for their faith in the system and for the valuable feedback they shared. Special thanks to Eduardo Manchón and Fátima Rodríguez Calvo for their willingness to try out the early versions of GIST and for their important insights and feedback. I'd also like to thank Daniel Kaeser, Sivan Hermon, Yuval Pemper, Oriol Sole, Tamar Schultz, Patric Fornasier, Fernando Diaz, Justas Kriukas, and Mattias Suter for their thoughtful input and suggestions.

Felipe Castro, thank you for your ongoing encouragement and for the deep discussions over the content and the target audience. Your broad knowledge and expertise in OKR, outcomes, and many other topics related to product development made this book better.

Thanks also to Jeff Gothelf, Joshua Seiden, and Victoria Olsen for their feedback on the article that preceded this book and for their encouragement to write a full book. Jeff also reviewed parts of the early version of this book.

Special mention to Rob Fitzpatrick who through his always-helpful advice and the information he shared in the Write Useful Books community, helped me learn the mechanics of writing, editing, and publishing a book.

I'm grateful to Marty Cagan and April Danford for their useful insights. Their combined advice helped me improve the message and guided me to pivot more heavily into evidence.

Thanks to Ronnie Kohavi whose articles and book inspired me, and for the expert feedback he shared on controlled experiment and on the book overall.

To my editor Jonathan Norman, thank you for the level-headed feedback, the guidance, and the constant encouragement that helped me push through. Thanks also to Peter Economy who helped me kick off this project and produce the first version of the manuscript.

A special thank you to all the beta readers that took the time to read versions of the book and give me feedback. I made hundreds of improvements, big and small thanks to your help. A partial list includes: Marc Abraham, Pierric Descamps, Matan Grady, Nacho Bassino, Donald Cox, Joseph Levin, Valentin Rabinovich, Phil Hornby, Kristian Bysheim, Jeroen Kemperman, Zsofia Kerekes, Claudia Pereyra, Silvan Geser, Gilad Katz, Berend van Niekerk, and Benjamin Simatos.

About the Author

Itamar Gilad is an author, speaker, and coach specializing in evidence-guided product management and product strategy. For over two decades he held senior product management and engineering roles at Google, Microsoft and a number of startups. At Google Itamar was first a product manager for YouTube and then led parts of Gmail.

Itamar publishes a popular product management newsletter—High Impact Product Management—and is the creator of a number of product management methodologies including the GIST Framework and the Confidence Meter. He is a regular speaker at product industry events and podcasts. To learn more about what Itamar does see itamargilad.com.

Index

Made in the USA
Middletown, DE
27 December 2024